HINDUISM
An Introduction

To my late grandfather
Dr. C. P. RAMASWAMI AIYAR
who first introduced me to the beauty
of Vedanta
and to my grandsons
PRASHANTH and RUDRA
hoping they will find the study of Hinduism
an exciting adventure

Cover Page
The Child Krishna playing his divine flute
Thanjavur painting

1
Young Krishna conquers the serpent king,
Kaliya
Bronze from Tamil Nadu

HINDUISM
An Introduction

Shakunthala Jagannathan

Vakils, Feffer and Simons Ltd.
Hague Building, 9, Sprott Road, Ballard Estate, Mumbai-400 001.

Credits

Book designed by **Zehra Tyabji**

Coloured Paintings published
with the permission and courtesy of:
C. R. Pattabhi Raman (Cover Page, Nos. 22, 46)
Aparna Art Gallery, Madras (Nos. 4, 59, 60)
A. R. Jagannathan (No. 6)

Colour Photography by **S. R. Rajagopal**

Drawings (Nos. 5, 9, 13, 18, 29, 31, 40, 44, 48, 50, 51, 54, 56, 57, 66)
by **Digamber Bhagat**

Black and white photographs and line drawings
published with the permission and courtesy of:
Archaeological Survey of India (Copyright with ASI)
(Nos. 1, 3, 7, 8, 14, 17, 27, 33, 38, 42, 43, 47, 49, 52, 53, 55)

Prince of Wales Museum, Mumbai
(Nos. 8, 10, 11, 12, 15, 16, 23, 24, 25, 26, 28, 30, 34, 39, 41, 45, 58)

Mafatlal Industries Ltd. and **Associated Companies,**
Mumbai
(Nos. 19, 20, 21, 61, 74, 78, 79, 80, 81, 82, 83, 85, 87)

Vivekananda Kendra, Madras
(Nos. 64, 65, 67, 70, 71, 73, 77, 84, 86, 89)

Bharatiya Vidya Bhavan, Mumbai
(Nos. 36, 75, 76)

Copyright © 1984 by Vakils, Feffer and Simons Ltd.
All rights reserved

First Printing 1984
Second Printing 1984
Third Printing 1985
Fourth Printing 1989
Fifth Printing 1991
Sixth Printing 1992
Seventh Printing 1994
Eighth Printing 1995
Ninth Printing 1996
Tenth Printing 1999

Price: Rs. 125/-

Published by Mrs. Jean Trindade
for Vakils, Feffer and Simons Ltd.
Hague Building, 9, Sprott Road, Ballard Estate
Mumbai-400 001, India

Printed by Arun K. Mehta at Vakil & Sons Ltd.
Industry Manor, Appasaheb Marathe Marg, Worli,
Mumbai-400 025, India

ISBN 81-87111-19-4

Contents

Preface

Some three years ago, a friend mentioned that his relatives living abroad wanted a simple but comprehensive book on Hinduism for their grown-up children, but he could not find one. I also agreed that foreign visitors to our country often asked for a guide book on the Hindu religion which they could understand and relate to what they saw in India. "Why don't you write one?" he asked, and from that was sown the germ of an idea.

Two years of research convinced me of the need for such a book, preferably illustrated (as none of the books in English covering all aspects of Hinduism is illustrated). However, attempting to trace the thread connecting seemingly contradictory beliefs of this ancient religion and transcribing it into book form was easier said than done. The greatest problem I faced was to decide what to leave out of this ocean known as Hinduism, so as to keep my book as brief as possible.

In this process several persons gave me invaluable help and I am deeply indebted to them. To mention a few to whom I owe eternal gratitude . . . .

Jagadguru Shri Jayendra Saraswathi, the Shankaracharya of Kanchi, for encouraging me to write such a book . . . .

To all those scholars, savants and men of religion whose books and studies guided my thinking . . . .

To my father C. R. Pattabhi Raman, and friend, Navnitbhai Parekh, for their valuable suggestions on additions and deletions . . . .

To Vimala Krishnamurti, who burnt midnight oil with me researching old scriptures, my mother Saraswathi, for the wealth of her Puranic lore, and my daughter, Nanditha Krishna, for vetting iconographical references . . . .

To Page Mehta, R. Subbu, columnist RGK, and my uncle, P. C. Sekhar, for going through the manuscript . . . .

To all those who assisted me in obtaining illustrations . . . . . .

To T. S. Jaya, Ashok Sapre, P. A. Padmanabhan and S. Narayan for their valuable assistance . . . .

And last but not the least, to G. U. Mehta and Arun and Sudha Mehta of Vakils for publishing this book . . . .

To all of them and to many more, and to the Divine Will which prevented my giving up half-way (as I was often tempted to!), I am ever beholden.

Shakunthala Jagannathan

March 1984

Kasturi Building

Mumbai-400 020

Blessings of

His Holiness Jagadguru Shri Jayendra Saraswathi, the Shankaracharya of Kanchi Kamakoti Peetam

This book on Hinduism fulfils an important need of the hour for our people and is particularly necessary for our youth. It brings forth the greatness and the sanctity of Hinduism for popular reading in a manner acceptable to Hindu ideals. The scope of this work includes such varied aspects of the religion as Nirguna Brahman, Saguna Brahman, the visualisation of the Hindu Trinity, Brahma-Vishnu-Shiva, the establishment of the six paths of worship by Adi Shankara and the duties of the householder.

The theory of reincarnation, release from the cycle of birth and rebirth, Prarabdha Karma, Samchita Karma and Agami Karma, the concept of Dharma, the four ashramas, Brahmacharya, Grihastha, Vanaprastha, and Sanyasa, and the six enemies of man — kama, krodha, lobha, moha, mada and matsarya, are dealt with in this illustrated book in simple language.

The clear explanations of Truth, Ahimsa, Vairagya, Purity, Self-control, and the three paths of attaining the Brahman, viz. by Bhakti Yoga, Karma Yoga or Jnana Yoga would, no doubt, benefit all readers, young as well as old, and scholars as well as the uninitiated.

We are very happy about the publication of this book.

May the writer continue with such good deeds which will benefit the people of our land.

(Translated from the original Tamil)

² Entrance to Hindu Temple, Bali, Indonesia

Hinduism is the oldest religion in the world and is the faith of over four-fifths of the diverse peoples of the vast sub-continent of India, of the people of Nepal and Bali (Indonesia) and of millions of Indians who have migrated overseas. There are, besides, many ancient cultures, as in South-East Asia, which have been greatly influenced by the Hindu cultural ethos.

The history of the Hindus, as we know it today, goes back 5000 years, but Hindus believe that their religion is without beginning or end and is a continuous process even preceding the existence of our earth and the many other worlds beyond. Science today accepts that there may be other worlds in the vast Universe, each with its own laws. Hindus have held this view from time immemorial.

The word Hindu is of geographic origin and was derived from the name originally given to the people settled on the River Sindhu. It was corrupted by foreign visitors to the word 'Hindu', and the faith of the Hindus was given the name 'Hinduism' in the English language. Scholars however call this the Brahmanical faith, for, as we shall show later, to attain the Brahman or the Universal Soul is the ultimate aim of all Hindu thought.

Philosophic thinkers of recent times do not like to describe Hinduism as a mere religion as they feel that this narrows it down and does not bring out adequately its great qualities of catholicity of outlook and free thinking, as even an atheist is not precluded from being a Hindu and no hell nor doomsday envisioned for the agnostic. It is therefore called Sanatana Dharma or the Eternal Religion. Others call it a fellowship of religions from its liberal absorption of the faiths of others.

The greatness of Hinduism is at once its complexity and its simplicity, and the fact that it permeates totally the life of every Hindu from the moment of his birth, be he a believer or non-believer, a scholar or an illiterate. It is for this reason that it is often said that Hinduism is not just a religion but a way of life.

It is important to realise, before we delve further, that Hinduism is a rare faith with few "do's" and "don'ts" postulated, but one which has many signposts showing the different spiritual paths available to different types of people. It accepts the reality that there are varying intellectual and spiritual levels in each one of us and all cannot therefore take the same path, although the goal may be the same. Hinduism therefore offers different approaches to persons of different aptitudes, depending on whether he be a philosopher or a poet, a mystic or a man of action, an intellectual or a simple man of faith. This is a unique feature of the religion as it permits the greatest of freedom of worship and insists that each person must be guided by his or her own individual spiritual experience. It does not accept dictatorship in religious guidance.

Another quality unique to Hinduism is its tremendous tolerance of other religious faiths and beliefs. In the Bhagavad Gita, an important scripture of Hinduism, Lord Krishna, worshipped as an incarnation of Lord Vishnu himself, says, "Whosoever follows any faith and worships me under whatsoever denomination in whatsoever form with steadfastness, his faith shall I indeed reinforce". Most other religions say, "Your religion is wrong and to follow it is a sin. Get converted to my religion and Heaven will be yours". The Lord worshipped by the Hindus implies in effect, "Come to me as a Hindu, Christian, Muslim or Sikh. I shall make you a better Hindu, Christian, Muslim and Sikh". Conversion to Hinduism (minimal as it is) has therefore never been through force or wars, nor as a result of bigotry or by temptations offered to the economically weak, nor does bringing about conversions confer any special spiritual benefits.

Hinduism, again unique amongst religions, allows a Hindu to worship in a church, mosque or gurdwara as freely as he does in a temple. Very few religious faiths have such a tolerant approach nor would their priests or religious heads permit it.

Hinduism has attracted thinkers from all over the world through the ages, and today there is a great thirst for knowledge of this faith which is practical enough to permit social change and scientific progress, yet highly philosophical and sublime, aiming at ethical perfection. However it is most unfortunate that today even educated Hindus are often unaware as to what the religion teaches or stands for, or what its fundamental beliefs are.

This ignorance can be traced to the breaking up of the joint family system in urban areas. In small towns and villages, where it still exists, all members of a family headed by a patriarch live under one roof, and the young are taught all aspects of their religion by grandparents, both in the form of stories and by precept. Today most young people growing in urban surroundings are not aware as to what Hinduism is, as few parents spare the time to teach them the fundamental beliefs of their faith. What is often picked up by the young are superstitions which have nothing to do with the religion, while their parents perform rites and rituals periodically without understanding their symbolism or even the meaning of the *mantras* or prayer chants that go with them. The freedom permitted by this faith, which does not even ask for a weekly visit to a temple, has been misused, leading to widespread ignorance of what it stands for.

An attempt is therefore being made in this book to briefly mention the main groups of scriptures of the Hindus and to explain the main tenets and beliefs of one of the most ancient people of this earth. To do so in one volume and a small one at that, and to condense scriptures of hundreds and thousands of pages into half-a-page or one page are onerous tasks, but are unavoidable if a total picture of the religion is to be given in the briefest form possible. If the continuous thread running through and binding seemingly contradictory beliefs of this faith can be clearly discerned, then my task would not have

been in vain. To make it easier for the reader, the meanings of
Indian words are given in the text itself. The Glossary contains
some of the popular words used with simplified pronunciations.

This study is not a comprehensive one nor the final word on the
subject. It is hoped that it will whet the appetite of the readers
to go to the originals and study for themselves the truths of one
of the great religions of the world. Equally important, I hope it
will serve as a short introduction to the foreign visitor before he
or she finds more comprehensive studies on a subject which is
as brilliant as the sunrises of our great land, whose scriptures
are as poetic as its sunsets and whose faith is as tolerant as the
gentle smile of this beautiful earth which has always cherished
and welcomed the visitor, sending him back the wiser for his
visit, even while partaking of the wisdom that he brings with
him to our shores.

3
Standing Ganesha in bronze
Thirupalaivanam, Tamil Nadu

4
Saraswati, Goddess of Learning and Wisdom
4 Thanjavur painting

Hinduism is not based on any single book nor on the words of any single teacher or prophet. It is based on the Eternal Truth.

However there are, literally, thousands of books and scriptures to guide both the beginner and the scholar, verily a cornucopia of spiritual literature.

The Srutis

The first set of books, which are the primary authority or the very soul of Hinduism, are known as "Sruti", meaning that which has been heard or revealed. These Srutis are known as the Vedas. The word 'Veda' is derived from the word *'vid'*, to know, and the Vedas are holy or spiritual knowledge of the Eternal Truth. The word 'Rishi' is derived from the word *'dris'*, to see. The Rishis were the Seers or Sages to whom the Vedas were revealed by Divine intervention and in whose hearts and minds they were heard. The Vedas are *apaurusheya* (of divine origin) and are unchangeable and eternal. They teach the highest truths ever known to man, and are valid for all time and all ages.

Hindus believe that Creation is *anadi* (that which has no beginning) and that it is eternal. At the end of each *kalpa* (a unit of time equal to a day of Brahma, the Creator, amounting to 4,320 million earth years), it exists in a subtle form in God, from whence each time is recreated a new Universe. At the end of the last age, there was a great deluge or *pralaya,* which destroyed the Universe. Brahma, the Creator, is believed to have meditated at the dawn of this age, called the Swetavaraha Kalpa, when the Great God appeared in the form of the sound of OM (ॐ) also known as the Pranava. (OM, as the symbol of the Absolute, is therefore the most sacred symbol of Hinduism.)

Brahma then prayed to Him for knowledge to create a new Universe. From the vibrations of the sound of OM (also spelt AUM), the Lord conceived the Rig Veda, the Yajur Veda, the Sama Veda and the Atharva Veda. The Great God then taught these four Vedas to Brahma who created our present Universe with this supreme knowledge received by him. In other words, the Vedas existed even before the creation of our universe.

Sage Veda Vyasa codified the four Vedas. His disciples, Paila, Vaisampayana, Jaimini and Sumanta taught them to their disciples and the latter, in turn, to their pupils. This is how the Vedas have come to us through thousands of years. They are therefore called *amnaya*, or that which has come to us by tradition.

The Rig Veda consists mostly of hymns in praise of the Divine, the Yajur Veda mainly of hymns used in religious rituals and rites, the Sama Veda of verses from the Rig Veda set to music, and the Atharva Veda guides man in his material and daily living.

The Vedas have several parts. They are the *mantra* (or hymns), the Brahmana (or the explanatory treatises for using *mantras* in rituals), the Aranyaka or forest books (which are the mystical interpretations of the *mantras* and rituals), and the Upanishad. The Upanishads are the most important part of the Vedas, as it is believed that knowledge of the Upanishads brings about the destruction of *avidya* or ignorance, one of the greatest failings of mankind.

There are about 108 Upanishads in all. Of these, 12 are the most important—the Isa, Kena, Katha, Prasna, Mundaka, Mandukya, Aitareya, Taittiriya, Chandogya, Brihadaranyaka, Kaushitaki and Svetasvatara.

The Upanishads reveal some of the greatest truths ever known to mankind. They contain the essence of the philosophy of the Vedas and the profound spiritual truths contained in them have blazed through the ages, guiding Man in his search for spiritual enlightenment.

5
Brahma in meditation and the vibrations of OM

6

Shiva as Nataraja, Lord of the Cosmic
Dance, with Parvati (as Shivakami), Vishnu
(as Govindaraja), Nandi and devotees
Thanjavur painting

The next set of books are the Upa Vedas or the Subsidiary Vedas, which are four in number. The first is Ayurveda, the science of extending life, including in its study the systems of maintaining good health and the use of medicines derived from herbs, roots and fruits. Highly developed in ancient India, this science of Indian medicine and pharmacology had the positive side of promoting health, the curative side consisting of the treatment of diseases, and a highly developed school of surgery. Many medicines of the ancient Hindus have since been adapted into the European medical system and are in use to this day.

Charaka, the greatest of ancient Hindu physicians, was possibly the first to speak of a code of ethics for the physician to treat patients without thought of gain or reward, and to keep in strict confidence the illness of a patient.

Sushruta, the great surgeon of ancient India, mentions 120 surgical instruments in use at that time. Plastic surgery was a well-developed science as was the art of setting right deformed parts of the body such as the ears, nose and lips. The latter skill was taken from India to the West by the surgeons of the British East India Company as late as in the 18th century.

The second Upa Veda is the Dhanurveda, the science of archery and the use of weapons. Even weapons like missiles are covered in this ancient treatise. However the rules of warfare were strictly laid down, and the use of such weapons was permitted only for the destruction of evil and for the protection of the physically weak, of sages in meditation, of holy men and mendicants, of women and children.

Even during warfare, rules and regulations were strictly observed. For example, opposing armies laid down their arms at sunset and dined together amicably, commencing hostilities only at sunrise the next day.

The third Upa Veda, the Gandharva Veda, is the science of music and dance. The sage Bharata has written the Natya Shastra, the oldest book in the world on this subject. He is believed to have been taught by Sage Tandu after the latter witnessed the cosmic dance of Lord Shiva.

The recitation of the Vedas, especially of the musical Sama Veda, placed great emphasis on musical notation and sound, and as they were learnt by rote by word of mouth, the science of sound and acoustics, with emphasis on musical chanting, reached high standards of perfection. The earliest musical octave was accurately divided into 22 quarter tones. Musical instruments of ancient India included a wide variety of percussion instruments (drums), wind instruments (such as the flute), and stringed instruments (such as the *vina*), many of which have survived to this day.

Music was considered a method of reaching God-head. The Veda of the Hindus and the Zend-Avesta of the Zoroastrian religion are the earliest known instances of words set to music.

7
Shiva performing the Tandava dance
Halebid, Karnataka

8

The fourth of this series of Upa Vedas is the Arthashastra. This is a treatise on polity, state administration, and the conduct of commerce.

We then have the Vedangas, the explanatory limbs of the Vedas. The first, called Siksha, was written by Sage Panini. It is the science of phonetics and also deals with pronunciation and accent.

Panini also authored another Vedanga, Vyakarana, the science of grammar. Panini's commentaries on this subject guide students of the Sanskrit language to this day.

The third Vedanga is Nirukta, the science of the etymology of the words in Vedic Mantras. It is the science of linguistics dealing with the formation and meanings of words.

The fourth, the Chandas Shastra, teaches prosody, the art of versification, and deals with the use of metres in prose and poetry.

The Kalpa Shastra deals with the science of rituals and ceremonials in religious rites.

The last Vedanga is Jyotisha, the science of astronomy and astrology. Knowledge of astrology was utilised in ancient India to fix auspicious timings for events of peace and war. It was only after the 6th century that this school of study gave importance to predictions on the future of individuals, which have become the craze today.

8
Marriage of Shiva and Parvati
Bronze from Thiruvenkadu, Tamil Nadu

The world owes much to Indian mathematics, which knowledge was conveyed to the Arab and the Greek worlds. The concept of zero (or *sunya*), abstract concepts of numbers, algebra, the decimal system, all owe their origin to the ancient Hindus. The Isavasya Upanishad taught, as a philosophical concept, the revolutionary mathematical truth that Infinity divided by any number continues to be Infinity.

Astronomy was the more important branch of the science of Jyotisha and the ancient Hindus, with their mathematical excellence, sent their advanced theories to Europe through the Greeks. Aryabhata, the ancient Indian astronomer, opined that it was not the sun that moved round the earth but the earth which, on its axis, rotated around the sun. Knowledge of the equinoxes, the movements of the sun and the moon, and fantastically accurate predictions of eclipses are evidence of the depth of study of the ancient astronomers. The open-air observatory at Jaipur with its minutely accurate instruments is an indication of what its precursors must have been.

The above books are part of the Srutis or the Vedas and are the first set of scriptures.

The Smritis

The second set are the Smritis, meaning that which is remembered. Unlike the Srutis, which are of Divine origin, the Smritis are human compositions which regulate and guide individuals in their daily conduct and list the codes and rules governing the actions of the individual, the community, society and the nation. They are known as the Dharma Shastras or the laws governing righteous conduct.

A day of Brahma the Creator is also known as a *kalpa,* and is divided into four ages or *yugas,* the Satya or Krita Yuga, the Treta Yuga, the Dwapara Yuga, and the present age, the Kali Yuga, which is also the age of degeneration of virtue. Each age has its own law-givers.

There are 18 Smritis in all and there have been many law-givers in the land, such as Manu, Yajnavalkya, Shankha, Likhita and Parashara.

Manu is the earliest of them all and his laws have greatly influenced the life of the people of this country. However, it is mainly on the Yajnavalkya Smriti that Hindu Law of today is based.

Hinduism is unique in that it accepts that the rules of society change with every age, and therefore the laws, or the Dharma Shastras, must change from time to time. Since these laws are enunciated for the guidance of Man, they are governed by the time and age he lives in. Hinduism is a living, practical religion because it accepts that the laws governing the conduct of man and society are man-made laws which have to be flexible and dynamic and subject to change. It therefore does not give room to bigotry or intolerance as it does not say that a set of rules made hundreds or thousands of years ago should be valid today.

This has made it possible for the laws relating to Hindu society to be further changed by legislation in modern times, for protecting the interests of women, of daughters and wives.

Both the Srutis and Smritis are read and memorised by scholars and were utilised by king and priest, by the rulers and their ministers, to implement Divine and Human Laws.

The Epics

However, since the ordinary people do not have the erudition to read and understand these books, there are a third set of books, the Itihasas or Epics, which serve the purpose. The profound philosophy of the Upanishads is presented in the form of parables and stories in these epics for the guidance of the common people.

The great epics of Hinduism are the Ramayana, the Mahabharata, the Yogavasishta and the Harivamsa. They are also called the Suhrit Samhitas or friendly compositions, as they teach the greatest of truths in an easy, friendly way without taxing the mind, as the language is simple and the contents easily understood.

9
Krishna's advice to Arjuna (the Bhagavad Gita)

11

Of these the Ramayana and the Mahabharata are known even to the most illiterate of Hindus as they have come down through the ages by word of mouth. They teach the ideals of Hinduism in a most understandable form and it is because of these books that the most illiterate of our peasants is not ignorant. On the other hand he carries within him the wisdom of the Upanishads which has been conveyed to him by these two major epics in story, ballad or dance form.

The more popular of these two epics is the Ramayana. Also known as the Adi Kavya or the first poetic composition of the world, it was written by the great sage, Rishi Valmiki. In this epic is given the story of Rama, believed to be an incarnation of Lord Vishnu, born on earth to show the path of righteousness.

10
Young Rama and Lakshmana accompany Sage Vishwamitra to the dwellings of ascetics
Mewar miniature, Rajasthan

Dasaratha, king of Ayodhya, had four sons, Rama, born of his first queen, Kausalya, Lakshmana and Shatrughna, born of his second queen, Sumitra, and Bharata, born of his favourite queen, Kaikeyi.

Rama was banished to the forest for 14 years at the behest of his step-mother, Kaikeyi, and left with his wife, Seeta, and brother, Lakshmana. In the forest Seeta was abducted by the demon-king, Ravana of Lanka. Rama, helped by an army of monkeys, and by Hanuman, the most loyal of them all, fought and destroyed Ravana and brought back Seeta. He was then crowned king and ruled over Ayodhya.

Rama Rajya, the reign of Rama, was one of idealism and perfection, when no tear was shed nor sorrow experienced. It was a time of peace and joy, an idyllic era for all good people. Ayodhya became a land where tolerance and understanding governed the actions of everyone and even the King's actions were subject to the will of the people. Ideal behaviour of the rulers and ruled, of men and women, were shown by the actions of the characters in this epic, thereby teaching the people, subtly yet effectively, what ideal behaviour should be.

For example, to show the qualities of ideal queens, we have Dasaratha's queens, Kausalya and Sumitra, soft-spoken but strong, who placed the prestige of the king and the kingdom above their love of their sons. Dasaratha had earlier given two boons to Kaikeyi and she asked that Rama be sent to the forest for 14 years and her own son, Bharata, be crowned king. Rama, the ideal son, readily agreed to go and Lakshmana accompanied him. Their mothers, Kausalya and Sumitra, sent away their beloved sons to the forest so that king Dasaratha could keep his word. A second lesson learnt from this was the importance of the spoken word, especially the promises made by a ruler.

11
Rama, Seeta and Lakshmana in the forest
Bundi miniature, Rajasthan

Also, the sacrifices of which Hindu women were capable were depicted by several such instances.

To delineate the qualities of a high-principled man, we have Bharata who, on his return from a visit to his uncle, found his brother banished to the forest by his mother and the kingdom his to be ruled, as his father had died of grief meanwhile. However he would not take over as king and, when Rama refused to come back till all 14 years of exile promised by him to his late father and step-mother were over, Bharata took his brother's *paduka* or wooden slippers, placed them on the throne and ruled as regent till his brother's return.

The qualities of the ideal man, prince and king are learnt by the ordinary people to this day from the character of Rama, of the ideal woman and wife from the strong but gentle character embodied in Seeta, and of the qualities of ideal brothers from the behaviour of Bharata, Lakshmana and Shatrughna.

12
Rama, Seeta and Lakshmana in the
hermitage of holy men
14   Kangra miniature, Himachal Pradesh

The ideal qualities of loyalty, unstinted devotion and love are depicted in the character of Hanuman, the monkey, who helped Rama cross over to Lanka and defeat Ravana. When Lakshmana was hit by a poison arrow and needed medicinal herbs from the Oshadhi Mountain in the Himalayas, Hanuman flew north all the way but found, on reaching there, that he could not identify the particular herb asked for. Knowing that his beloved Rama may not live if Lakshmana was not revived, he lifted the whole mountain and carried it all the way back to Lanka.

The potential for good and evil in all beings is brought out again and again. The destruction of evil by good either by oneself or by divine intervention is a constant theme of Hinduism.

13
Hanuman flying with the mountain of herbs to cure Lakshmana

Even the demons were not all bad and wicked and are shown as having good qualities also. Ravana, the demon-king of Lanka, was a great scholar. Even though he abducted Seeta to make her his queen, he treated her with respect and regard and never molested or harmed her but awaited her consent to marry her. Hanuman, in his attempt to locate Seeta, visits Lanka, and is greatly struck by Ravana and says, "What courage! What strength! What a combination of great qualities is Ravana!"

Ravana's brother, the demon Kumbhakarna, disapproved strongly of the abduction of Seeta. Yet because he had prospered under Ravana's patronage, and "eaten his salt", he refused to desert his brother in his hour of peril.

The great virtue of loyalty, even for a lost cause, was brought out by such instances.

Through the stories from the Ramayana which are recited to them, the ordinary people learn the difference between right and wrong, develop a high sense of values and understand what ideal behaviour is. The tremendous cultural heritage of the Vedas and Upanishads has reached and permeated to the most illiterate of our people through Sage Valmiki's priceless epic, the Ramayana. This is why our peasants, even those living in remote villages, know to this day what they can expect from the laws of the land and are not ignorant of their rights nor of what is due to the ruled by the rulers. The illiterate peasant trusts his rulers implicitly, expecting another Rama Rajya, and today uses the modern tool of the vote to express his feelings towards his rulers. The illiterate villager is therefore not ignorant as the city educated think him to be.

The second great epic of the Hindus, the Mahabharata, was compiled by Sage Vyasa and revolves around the Great War between two princely families, the righteous five Pandava brothers and their evil cousins, the hundred Kauravas. The central character of the epic is Lord Krishna, an incarnation of Vishnu on earth, a man of action and statesman.

When poised on the battlefield ready for battle, Arjuna, the great warrior and one of the Pandava brothers, sees that the enemies that are arrayed before him are his close relations, cousins, uncles and grand-uncles, and refuses to fight or destroy them. Krishna, who acts as his charioteer, advises him on the importance of his *dharma* or duty as a warrior to fight for righteousness. The Kauravas, representing evil, have to be destroyed to restore Dharma or righteousness in the land.

Swami Vivekananda compares the Kurukshetra battlefield to the world we live in. The five Pandava brothers represent righteousness and the hundred Kauravas the myriad worldly attachments we have to fight against. Arjuna, the soul awakened by the teachings of Krishna, is the general who leads in this battle.

The teachings of Lord Krishna called the Bhagavad Gita, or the Song of the Lord, are part of the discourse between Lord Krishna and Arjuna at Kurukshetra during the great

Mahabharata War. In this priceless scripture, Lord Krishna places emphasis on Nishkama Karma or action without desire or passion and without any worry about the fruits or results of one's actions. Through such scriptures the duties of the ideal man were laid down, showing him to be a Yogi, or one unattached to worldly desires, as far as his heart and mind are concerned, but also as a man of action setting right the wrongs of society.

An interesting allegory is the comparison of the Upanishads to a cow, the Bhagavad Gita to milk, Krishna to a cowherd and Arjuna to a calf. In other words, the essence of the Upanishads is milked by Krishna and the milk, the Bhagavad Gita, fed to Arjuna.

The Shantiparva of the Mahabharata contains the teachings of Bhishma Pitamaha, the grand-uncle of the family from which were descended both the Pandavas and the Kauravas. These words of wisdom were uttered while Bhishma was awaiting his death after being seriously wounded in the Great War. In his discourse, Bhishma instructs Yudhishtira, the oldest Pandava brother, on Dharma or righteous conduct and duty, on statecraft and the responsibilities of a ruler. These teachings on Hindu Dharma are without parallel.

From the Mahabharata, therefore, the people learnt the rules and the codes of ideal conduct laid down for man and woman, king and commoner.

14
Venugopala Krishna, the protector of cattle, playing the flute
Somnathpur, Karnataka

15
Fight between Bhima the Pandava and
Duryodhana the Kaurava in the
Mahabharata war
Moghul miniature

16
The dying Bhishma on a bed of arrows with
Krishna and the Pandavas
Moghul miniature

19

The Puranas

After the Srutis, Smritis and Itihasas, we have the fourth set of books, the Puranas. There are 18 Puranas (of which the Bhagavata, Vishnu and Markandeya Puranas are most popular) and 18 subsidiary or Upa Puranas. They are not meant for the scholar, the intellectual or the spiritually evolved, but consist of tales which convey the truths of the Vedas and Dharma Shastras in the form of short stories. Told to children, to the simple villager and illiterate peasant, these imaginative stories have formed the very basis of the religious education of our ordinary people and help to teach them simple but fundamental truths of religion and morality, of what is right and wrong in behaviour.

These Puranas have been conveyed to successive generations by word of mouth, by grandmothers to their grandchildren, by the village priest and by the wandering minstrel. Walls of temples are covered with carvings of Puranic stories, a visual method for educating the ordinary people.

For example, to teach the people that God is everywhere and always comes to the help of His devotee, the story of Prahlada is told. Prahlada's father, the demon-king Hiranyakashipu, tried his best to teach his son that there was none more powerful than himself. But Prahlada was engrossed in his worship of the Lord. Hiranyakashipu shouted at his son—"Do not pray to any but me, Hiranyakashipu, the greatest of them all. I have a boon that neither man, beast nor weapon can kill me. Nor can I die inside or outside a house, at day-time or at night, on earth or in the sky. Where then is this God of whom you always speak? Let Him dare appear before me!"

But the child Prahlada insisted that God was everywhere, outside and within us and all around us.

"Is he in this pillar? If so let him come out and fight me or I will kill you". Saying this he struck the pillar.

Out of the pillar, which burst open, Vishnu appeared as Narasimha and destroyed evil in the form of the demon. Neither man nor beast killed Hiranyakashipu, but Vishnu did as Narasimha, half-man, half-lion. He killed him neither inside nor outside the palace but on the door-step, on the threshold. He was killed not by day or by night but at the hour of twilight. He did not kill him on the earth or in the sky but did so by placing him on his lap.

17
Narasimha destroying the demon,
Hiranyakashipu
Bronze from Srirangam, Tamil Nadu

20

This story taught that God is everywhere and finds some way to come to the aid of those devotees who place their total faith in him.

The Puranas taught the power of a chaste and good woman with stories like that of Savitri. Born the daughter of the King of Madra, Savitri chose Satyavan, the son of a deposed king, the blind Dyumatsena, as her husband. The couple lived with Satyavan's parents in the forest. Savitri knew from Sage Narada himself that Satyavan would die one year hence. On the day of his predicted death she followed him into the forest when he went out to cut wood, all the time worrying as to how she could prevent Death from taking him away.

By the power of her purity, Savitri saw Yama, the god of Death, take away Satyavan's *prana* or breath of life, and followed him. She pleased him greatly by her words of wisdom and got four boons given to her provided she did not ask for Satyavan's life. As the fourth boon, she asked for a hundred sons and Yama granted her wish.

She then asked Yama how she, a chaste woman, could bear sons when her husband was no longer alive. Not being able to go back on his word, which is considered one of the greatest of wrongs, Yama gave back Satyavan alive to Savitri.

18
Savitri and Satyavan with Yama, the god of Death, on his vehicle, the buffalo

21

Ignorant people often use the words 'Sati Savitri' to describe a weak self-effacing woman. On the contrary, Savitri was a strong and good woman who, by determination, could even overcome the dictates of Destiny.

The power of a good woman over gods and demons was an oft-repeated theme of the Puranas.

Princess Sukanya blinded an old sage, Rishi Chyavana, by accident. She then insisted on marrying him and looking after him, thereby sacrificing her life of luxury as a princess, and spending her hours caring for her old and blind husband.

Once the Ashwini twins, (who are celestial beings or Devas), saw the unparalleled beauty of Sukanya and wished to test her steadfastness and loyalty to the blind sage. They appeared in human form and asked her to marry one of them. When she refused, they took a wager with her stating that they would transform her husband into a young god to look exactly like themselves and if Sukanya did not identify him, she would have to marry one of them.

Sukanya got the divine inspiration that only the one who blinked and whose feet stood firmly on the ground was a mortal. By the power of her prayer she pointed out her husband and showed that, before the strength of a good woman, even the heavenly Ashwini twins were powerless. She is known as Sati Sukanya, Sati meaning a pure and chaste woman, and has become a symbol of the power of a good woman as, through her devotion, she restored the youth and eyesight of Sage Chyavana.

The story of Dhruva, a young prince who, by his constancy and meditation won the eternal blessings of Vishnu, was told in the Puranas to emphasise the importance of prayer and meditation and their power to move God. By his single-minded constancy and devotion to the Lord, Dhruva, after his death, was transformed into the only star in the Universe that stays unmoved, the Pole Star, known to this day as Dhruva in Hindu Astronomy.

19
Dhruva meditates on Vishnu

The story of Markandeya again showed how a young boy of sixteen conquered his pre-destined Fate by his devotion to Shiva. Given only a 16-year span of life, Markandeya did not allow Death to take him away on the due date but was given the gift of immortality by Shiva by the strength of his *bhakti* or devotion.

Even today when we bless a child when he sneezes, we say, "May you have the life-span of Markandeya!". These Puranic stories are so strongly intertwined in our daily lives and have been recounted as bed-time tales to Hindu children from time immemorial.

To teach children the importance of looking after their elders, we have the story of the young boy, Shravana, who denied himself the joys of childhood and boyhood while caring for his old and blind parents.

When they wished to go on a pilgrimage to holy cities, he placed them in bamboo baskets tied to a pole which he carried on his young shoulders and cheerfully undertook the journey at great discomfort to himself.

21
Markandeya worshiping the Shiva Lingam

The strong family ties of our peasants, the care they lavish on their elders (supporting them by working in cities, depriving themselves of even basic necessities and sending home a major part of their earnings), are evidence of the influence of such stories which deify filial ties.

20
Young Shravana carrying his blind parents   23

The coronation of Rama
Thanjavur painting

Another interesting Puranic story is that of King Usinara of the Sibi clan who was a great and just king whose generosity knew no bounds. Once when a dove rushed to him for help to escape a hawk, the king gave it protection. The hawk protested at being deprived of his rightful food.

The Sibi King offered his flesh as substitute, but however much he cut slices of flesh from his body, the weight of the dove was greater. Usinara then offered himself in entirety and balanced the scale.

Indra, the king of the Devas (celestial beings or lesser gods) and Agni, the god of Fire, had taken the form of the hawk and the dove only to test the generosity and justice of the Sibi King, Usinara. The virtue of placing generosity over and above one's life was taught by such stories.

Similarly, to teach the importance of adhering to Truth, there are stories such as that of King Harischandra. Wedded to Truth and true to a promise given by him, he gave away his kingdom. To repay a sum of money promised to Vishwamitra, he sold his beloved wife and son as slaves. Finally he sold himself to the keeper of a cremation ground to pay the last instalment of the amount promised. However Harischandra's sorrow knew no bounds when his wife Chandramati (known as Taramati in some parts of the country), brought the dead body of their son, Rohitsawa, for cremation.

When Harischandra and his wife decided to fall into the pyre with their son, Indra, the king of the Devas and Yama, the god of Death saved all three, and acknowledged that Harischandra's adherence to Truth was a lesson even to the gods.

The importance of Truth and the inviolability of the spoken word are therefore taught by many such stories from the Puranas.

Sudama (also known as Kuchela) was an impoverished Brahmin with innumerable children. He had been a childhood companion of Lord Krishna at Sage Sandeepani's hermitage. One day, when there was not a morsel of food in the house, his wife forced him to go to Krishna to get some help. The only gift he took to Krishna were a few handfuls of beaten rice, but was shy of giving this poor gift to the great Krishna, who, however, forced it out of his hand and ate a mouthful. When Sudama returned without having asked Krishna for any favours, he found his hut turned into a mansion and his family prosperous and happy.

The story of Sudama impressed on the people that the poorest gift when given with love is great enough to please God Himself. Also that true friendship cuts through barriers of inequalities of position and wealth.

It is again in the Puranas that we read of the ten incarnations or Avatars of Lord Vishnu on earth. These incarnations detail the help given by God during the various stages of Man's

23
Shiva and Yama (Markandeya episode)
Pattadakal, Karnataka

24
Indra and Indrani on the elephant, Airavata
Somnathpur, Karnataka

25

25
To save his people and cattle, Krishna
swallows the forest fire
Mewar miniature, Rajasthan

evolution by His appearing on earth in different forms.
Surprisingly, many of these incarnations coincide with modern
theories of evolution.

These Avatars teach mankind that God has re-established
Dharma or righteous justice and destroyed injustice from time
to time by appearing on earth in various incarnations.

Starting with the Matsya (fish) Avatar, Lord Vishnu has
appeared as Kurma (tortoise), Varaha (boar), Narasimha (half
man, half lion), Vamana (the dwarf), Parasurama (the angry
man), Rama (the perfect man), Krishna (the divine statesman)
and the Buddha (the compassionate man).

The first Avatar, that of Matsya the fish, was taken by Vishnu
at the end of the last *kalpa* or age, when there was a deluge that
destroyed the world that existed then. Choosing a sage, Rishi
Satyavrata, Lord Vishnu commanded him to gather together
the seven great sages, samples of all animals, birds, plants, and
seeds, and wait in a boat. The gigantic golden fish then dragged
the boat through the turbulent oceans all through the long,
long night of Brahma till the deluge ended and Brahma created
the present world. This Avatar is akin to the story of Noah's
Ark in the Old Testament, an evidence of the closeness in
many of the beliefs of ancient religions. Another version has it
that a demon once stole the four Vedas and hid them under the
sea. Vishnu took the form of a giant fish and retrieved
these scriptures.

In the Kurma Avatar, Vishnu took the form of a tortoise to help the Devas (heavenly beings or lesser gods), to obtain the nectar of immortality which the Asuras (demons) were also after. The Devas and Asuras churned the ocean to get this nectar, using the giant snake, Vasuki, as the churning rope and Mount Mandara as the churning rod. To prevent the mountain sinking into the ocean, Vishnu as a giant tortoise supported the mountain under water until the nectar of immortality emerged which Vishnu gave to the Devas alone.

At the end of the deluge in the last *kalpa* or age, Bhoomi Devi (Mother Earth) sank into the bottom of the ocean. Vishnu taking the form of a large boar, Varaha, dived into the ocean and carried the goddess out of the waters supported by his massive snout.

In order to destroy Bali, king of the demons, Vishnu took the Avatar of a midget, Vamana. He appeared during a huge *yajna* or sacrifice being conducted by the king when the latter was arrogantly distributing gifts to all who asked for it to show his power and wealth. Vamana asked for just three feet of land, measured by his own small feet. With the first foot he covered the earth, with the second, the heavens. When there

26
Vishnu as Varaha saving Mother Earth
Mahabalipuram, Tamil Nadu

27
Vamana as Trivikrama expands to cover the Universe
Namakkal, Tamil Nadu

was no place for the next foot of land, Bali, to show that he never went back on his word, offered his head. Lord Vishnu sent him to the nether regions but glorified this act unto eternity.

When the kings of the earth became autocratic and started to harm ordinary people and sages in the forest, Vishnu took the Avatar of Parasurama and destroyed all the Kshatriyas (princes) who were harassing the people.

When priesthood became arrogant and priests used rituals to exploit the people, Vishnu took the Avatar of the Buddha to purify Hindu practices of excessive ritualism. He taught that all sorrow stemmed from attachments and desires and advocated a Middle Path consisting of the eight-fold virtues of right views, right resolve, right speech, right conduct, right livelihood, right effort, right mindfulness and right meditation.

The Avatars of Narasimha, Rama and Krishna have been explained earlier.

Hindus believe that at the end of this age, or Kali Yuga, there will be a holocaust of fire when the last Avatar, that of Kalki, will ride forth to save mankind and re-establish Dharma, or righteousness.

To summarise, we have covered four sets of books or scriptures so far. The first, the Srutis or the Vedas are the very soul of Hinduism and are of divine origin. They are eternal and without beginning or end. The Smritis or Dharma Shastras are like the body, subject to decay and can be changed from time to time, from age to age.

The truths of the Srutis and Smritis are conveyed to the ordinary people through the great Epics, which appeal to their hearts, and through the Puranas, which appeal to their imagination.

The Agamas

The fifth set of scriptures are the Agamas. These lay down the separate theological disciplines and doctrines for the worship of particular deities. Details of this type of worship will be covered later on. Suffice it to say now that from these Agamas have sprouted the three main sects amongst the Hindus, the Shaiva, Vaishnava, and Shakta.

The Shaiva Agama has led to the school of philosophy called Shaiva Siddhanta in the south, and to the Pratyabhijna system of Shaivism of Kashmir. In this Agama, the Supreme God is worshipped and adored under the different names and forms of Shiva.

Similarly, there are two main schools in the Vaishnava Agama, the Pancharatra and the Vaikhanasa, both of which glorify Vishnu. Of these the former is more popular and it is believed that this Agama was revealed by the Great God Himself in the form of Vishnu.

28
The Buddha
Bronze from Nagapattinam, Tamil Nadu

The Shakta Agama glorifies Devi, the consort of Shiva, as the World Mother who, as Shakti, is the energy-giving power behind all Creation, Creativity and Destruction.

The Tantric cult owes its origin to the Tantras and not to the Vedas (and therefore is not Hindu), but in the later period of Hindu history, Tantrics started to claim allegiance to the Shakta Agama. Many occult and magical practices trace their origin to Tantric worship as does much of the erotic art that we see on the walls of some temples to this day. However the Tantric cult was never fully accepted by Hinduism nor by the more important Hindu philosophers.

This set of scriptures, the Agamas, guide the faithful who are moved by their devotion to the Supreme God to worship one of His manifestations.

29
Shiva as Yogi

30
Durga slaying the buffalo demon,
Mahishasura, symbol of ignorance
Thane, Maharashtra

Each Agama, in turn, has several sections. The first part consists of the philosophy and spiritual knowledge behind the worship of the deity. The second part covers the Yoga and the mental discipline required for each school of worship.

An important part of the third section in each Agama covers the rules for constructing temples. That is why, whatever the style of outward architecture, the plan of temples is the same in whatever part of the country a temple is situated. Some are more elaborate than others with the addition of *mandapas* or halls, but the basic plan is the same, as laid down in each Agama for accommodating the rituals in that form of worship. Worship, even in temples, is individual, not congregational, which explains the small-sized *sanctum sanctorum* and narrow paths for circumambulation (walking around the shrine, chanting prayer hymns).

Equally important in the third section are the rules for sculpting or carving figures of deities and divinities. Even details such as the way Rama holds his bow, the length of his arms, the graceful stance of Seeta are written down so that, in whichever part of this vast country a temple is built, these rules are followed. The only differences are in the facial features of the images which are usually patterned on the racial characteristics of the local population.

The fourth part of the Agamas consists of the rules pertaining to the observances of religious rites and rituals at home and in the community, and in the observance of religious festivals. These are given in great detail, which explains their being observed from one end of the country to the other, with only local cultural variations.

The most beautiful aspect of the Agamas is the tremendous amount of poetic compositions and devotional songs that have sprung up under the shade of these theological scriptures in all the languages of the country. They have added greatly to the richness of the poetry and literary genius of our great land.

The Darshanas

The sixth or the last set of scriptures are the six Darshanas (meaning visions) which are schools of philosophy. These are for the intellectuals and the scholars who have six main schools of philosophic thought to guide them. They are Nyaya founded by Gautama Rishi, Vaiseshika by Kanada, Sankhya by Kapila Muni, Yoga by Patanjali, Mimamsa by Jaimini and Vedanta by Badarayana (Vyasa).

The philosophy of Nyaya is guided by pure logic and reasoning. Although this system itself is not popular today, its emphasis on logic and *tarka* or debate, has influenced all thinking in India through the ages.

The Vaiseshika school is the earliest in the world to talk of the universe as consisting of countless atoms each with its own *visesha* or particular quality. The Nyaya and Vaiseshika doctrines merge into one another and are studied together.

The Sankhya system also emphasises logic and inference but its main belief is that the universe consists of two elements,

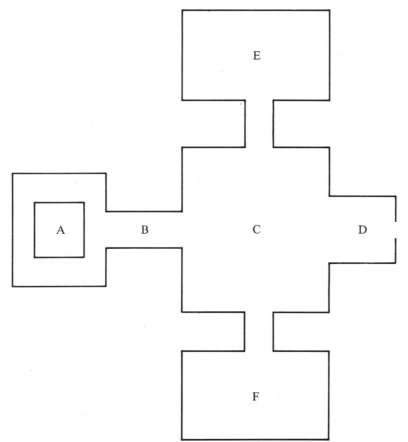

32
Basic Lay-out of a Hindu Temple

A — the *garbha griha* (or womb cell) where the image of the deity is installed. There is a passage for circumambulation around it.
B — *Antarala* or vestibule.
C — *Mandapa* or pillared hall where devotees gather for worship.
D — *Ardha Mandapa* or entrance porch.
E — Maha mandapa, a large hall used for discourses, *bhajans* (religious music sessions) etc.
F — *Kalyana Mandapa* where festivals and rituals, like the marriage of the deity, are conducted.
(E & F are found only in the larger temples, which often have several more *mandapas* and shrines.)

33
One of the *gopurams* or gateways of the
Meenakshi Temple
Madurai, Tamil Nadu

34
Lingaraj Temple
Bhubaneshwar, Orissa

purusha and *prakriti* (spirit and matter). It is the oldest school of all and mention is made of it in the Mahabharata.

The Yoga school accepts Sankhya philosophy but uses the system of mind control as the means of attaining God-head.

Mimamsa places great emphasis on Vedic rituals and sacrifices. (*Yajna,* the ritual of sacrifice, does not mean animal sacrifice, as is often misunderstood, but means the chanting of the Vedas while melted butter *(ghee),* grain and other offerings are poured into the sacred fire.)

Vedanta, meaning the end of the Vedas, bases its doctrine on the Upanishads. Of the six schools of philosophy, it is considered the most valid for the times we live in. For example, it teaches that the Supreme God can be reached only by one's own individual spiritual experience. Such a school of thought is more acceptable to the modern mind.

Each Veda has a Karma Kanda dealing with rituals, Upasana Kanda dealing with worship, and Jnana Kanda dealing with spiritual knowledge. Of the six schools, Vedanta holds that the Jnana Kanda or the path of knowledge is all-important and the other paths are merely steps to the final goal.

Vedanta insists on strict adherence to Truth and to tireless investigation. Thousands of years ago our ancients taught what is today in conformity with the modern scientific approach. The Manduka Upanishad says, "The path to the Divine is through Truth. Victory lies only with Truth. Untruth can never win". This emphasis on truth, investigation and individual spiritual experience makes Vedanta a philosophy appealing to the young and to the old. It is eternal and is applicable to all peoples and races of the thinking world.

All thinking in India has been affected by Vedanta which, even though we may not be aware of it, is the very root of our culture and beliefs. The Upanishads, the Vedanta Sutras and the Bhagavad Gita are called the Prasthana Traya, or the three authoritative scriptures of Hinduism. The three great commentators on the Vedanta Sutras were Adi Shankara, Ramanuja and Madhvacharya.

Vedanta has influenced great thinkers from time immemorial. Greek thinkers like Plato and later European philosophers like Spinoza, Nietzche and Schophenhauer were influenced by Vedantic philosophy as expounded by the ancient Rishis of the Upanishadic period, as have been philosophers all over the world through the ages, some subtly others overtly.

Vedanta appeals to the mind and to one's logical understanding. It gives satisfactory answers to the spiritual doubts of wise men at all times in all ages. It is a school of philosophy that appeals equally to the mystical minds of the Seers of the East, and to the philosophers of the Western world who are conditioned by a pragmatic and scientific environment.

36
Shri Ramanuja

The Tenets and Beliefs of Hinduism Chapter III

Hinduism, as we have seen, has a wealth of scriptures to guide both the initiate and the scholar. We now come to some of the fundamental tenets of the religion, as given in these scriptures.

Nirguna Brahman, the Absolute

The first question the Hindu is asked is whether he believes in God. Verily Hindus believe in the One God, Who, in His highest form is known as the Brahman, the Absolute, or the Universal Soul. He is immanent, within and about us, as also transcendent, outside material existence, transcending Time and Space. He is Nirguna, or without shape and form, and without beginning or end.

To explain that God exists and is reality, we have, in the Chandogya Upanishad, the illuminating story of the young Svetaketu's discussions on the Brahman with his father, Uddalaka Aruni, when he wanted to know where there was proof that God, who is not visible, really exists.

The father asked his son to get a fruit from the great *nyagrodha* (banyan) tree and to break it open. Taking one of the tiny seeds inside the fruit, he asked him to split it further, but young Svetaketu found nothing inside the seed. Yet, the father explained to him, inside the seed, not visible to the eye, is something out of which grows the mighty banyan tree. That same great power pervades the entire universe. It may not be seen, but It exists.

Uddalaka further asked his son to mix salt in water. After it had dissolved, he asked Svetaketu to taste the different parts of the water in the bowl and to separate the salt from the water. The son found all parts of the water equally salty and pointed out that the salt could not be separated from the water.

Uddalaka explained to Svetaketu that just as the salt pervades every drop of water in the cup, the Universal Spirit pervades all life.

Uddalaka also pointed out to his son that, just as the salt cannot be separated from the water, when finally all beings merge with the Brahman, they lose their individual entities, as the separate waters of rivers lose their separate forms when they flow into the ocean. Individuals may die but the Universal Spirit is deathless and life itself therefore does not die.

The Upanishads therefore teach us that the whole Universe is a manifestation of the Brahman. Life in all its forms is evolved from this single source of Energy, the Universal Spirit, which pervades all life and all things animate and inanimate. Since It is Nirguna or formless, the Brahman is not considered either male or female and is referred to by the impersonal pronoun, Tat (meaning That).

The Brahman is also described as "Satchitananda". Sat is that which exists (Being), Chit is pure intelligence (Consciousness), and Ananda is pure joy (Bliss).

All meditation begins with the words, "Om Tat Sat", to remind us of the only Ultimate Reality, the Brahman, which is the highest intelligence and is supreme bliss.

The mystic syllable, "OM" (pronounced "Ohm"), is known as the Pranava and is the symbol of the Brahman. This sacred word encompasses in itself the whole universe, the past, present and future and goes beyond the periphery of Time itself. Being the symbol of the Brahman or the Universal Soul, it is the very essence of all that is sacred in Hindu thought. It is used at the beginning of meditation, at the beginning and end of prayer, during the practice of Yoga, in fact at all times when the thought of the Brahman pervades one's being.

37
OM, the symbol of the Absolute

Saguna Brahman, The Great God

To ordinary mortals the Nirguna Brahman (without form or attributes) is impersonal and hard to comprehend. Therefore, in relation to the world and to make the Universal Spirit easily understandable, we have the Saguna Brahman, or the Brahman with form and attributes who is known as the One Great God or Ishwara. To those less developed spiritually and to the average man and woman, the concept of God has to be one with a form, a sort of Superior Being in human form on whom one can fix one's mind, especially during prayer.

The Trinity

The three main functions of God-head, Creation, Preservation and Destruction, are further simplified by the One Great God, Ishwara, being called Brahma, when He takes over the Creation of the Universe, Vishnu, when He assumes the role of the Preserver, and Shiva, when He is the Destroyer.

38
Brahma, Shiva, Vishnu, the Trinity
Halebid, Karnataka

A high degree of symbolism has been evolved to explain the attributes and qualities of God-head to the masses.

Different iconographical features are depicted for the different deities at different times, depending on the roles they perform. In one temple Vishnu may be shown in a peaceful form and in another in a role destroying evil. The weapons he holds could differ in these two forms. However a few of the major depictions are given below.

Brahma the Creator, for example, is shown with four heads facing all four directions symbolising that he has created the entire Universe. The fact that, after each *kalpa* (or age), he meditates and recreates the Universe we live in is symbolised by the Vedas he holds in his hand which guide him, and the *kamandalu* or vessel which is used in the ritual of prayer prior to *tapasya* (meditation and penance), after which he creates the Universe. He sits on a lotus which is a symbol of purity, as the lotus usually grows in muddy waters but is untouched by the dirt and mire from which it emerges. So also the true Yogi (one who practises Yoga and is an evolved being), should be unaffected by the world around him. To emphasise the closeness of Creation and Preservation, Brahma is shown emerging from the navel of Vishnu, the Preserver.

The feminine aspect of the Creator is personified in the beautiful form of Saraswati, the consort of Brahma, who is the embodiment of learning and wisdom. In her hand she holds the *vina,* symbolic of R'ta, the order in the Cosmic Universe and of Nada-Brahmam, the music or rhythm of the Universe. It is out of the sound of OM that the Universe was created. The hum or Nada, or the Inner Sound, the Music of the Cosmos, is also called the Music of the Spheres.

39
Brahma
Aihole, Karnataka

The beads in her fingers bring out the importance of prayer and meditation, and the palm leaf scrolls she holds represent learning and wisdom without which man is nothing. Her saree, always white, reminds us that all knowledge of value should be pristine pure and unsullied by untruth. She sits either on the pure lotus or on the peacock, in the latter case to remind us that the ego (symbolised by the peacock) is to be suppressed. The graceful swan is also her vehicle, to remind us to separate the chaff from the grain of true knowledge, just as the swan removes the water from milk before consuming the latter.

40
Saraswati, Consort of Brahma

Vishnu is represented as lying on the many-headed cobra, Ananta, in the ocean of milk. Ananta denotes cosmic energy and the ocean symbolises *ananda* or the endless bliss and grace of the Brahman. Vishnu is given the colour blue to symbolise Infinity, as he is as limitless as the blue sky. He holds the *chakra* or discus in one hand denoting that he maintains Dharma (righteousness) and order in the Universe. The *shankha* or conch that he holds in the other hand is for the removal of ignorance and is also symbolic of Nada-Brahmam or the Music of the Cosmos, as the conch when placed to the ear has a deep humming sound. The *gada* or mace is for removing the evil in the world and the lotus is the symbol of the beauty and purity of the Cosmic Universe. The vehicle of Vishnu is Garuda, the man-eagle, a figure of great strength, power and piety.

The feminine aspect of the Preserver is Lakshmi, the consort of Vishnu. The grace of God is personified in her as one who brings prosperity. One hand she holds in the *abhaya mudra* (with the hand held open with the palm facing the devotee and the fingers facing upwards) which says "Do not fear" and the other in the *varada mudra* (with the hand with the palm facing the devotee but with the fingers facing downwards) symbolic of the prosperity and grace she gives to the human race. She sits on the lotus and holds lotus flowers in her hand emphasising the importance of pure living without which her grace and giving are meaningless and prosperity but an empty shell.

Bhoo Devi, or Mother Earth, is depicted as the second consort of Vishnu.

41
Vishnu lying on the many-headed cobra,
Ananta (Sesha)
Aihole, Karnataka

42
Vishnu and Lakshmi on Garuda the eagle,
the vehicle of Vishnu
Halebid, Karnataka

43
Bronze Garuda
Tamil Nadu

40

Shiva, the Destroyer of the Universe, is often shown as Nataraja, the King of Dancers, his dance depicting Cosmic Energy. He dances on the demon, Apasmara Purusha, who represents our egos. Only by destroying one's ego can one attain God-head. In one hand Shiva holds a deer which denotes man's unsteady mind which darts hither and thither like the deer but has to be brought under control. In another he holds a rattle-drum, the symbol of creative activity, and in the third, the fire, the symbol of destruction. His fourth hand in the *abhaya mudra* says, 'Do not fear. I shall protect as I destroy'. The circle of fire behind him symbolises the continuity and eternal motion of the Universe through the paths of Creation, Preservation and Destruction. The river goddess Ganga, on Shiva's head, denotes eternity and purity, and the crescent moon reminds us of the waxing and waning of the Moon and the movement of Time. The cobra coiling around him is, again, the symbol of Cosmic Energy. Shiva's garland of skulls reminds man that death comes to all and his third eye depicts that God is all-seeing and wise. Placed in the centre of the forehead on which the Yogi concentrates while in meditation, this spot is symbolic as the seat of wisdom. Shiva opens his third eye to destroy evil.

45
Nataraja, Lord of the Dance
Bronze from Tamil Nadu

46
Shiva and Parvati on Shiva's vehicle, Nandi
the bull
Thanjavur painting

43

On the right ear Shiva wears a *kundala* (a jewel worn by men) and on his left ear a *tatanka* (ear ornament worn by women). This is to tell us that he is Ardhanarishwara, half-man and half-woman (as Parvati, his consort, is part of Shiva himself), symbolising the ideal union of man and woman. As fire and heat are inseparable, so are Shiva and Parvati one, and *purusha* (the spirit) and *prakriti* (matter) are combined in them.

The ashes worn by Shiva tell us that the body is transient and ends in ashes. The tiger-skin that he wears around his waist is the *ahamkara* or arrogant pride which, like the tiger, springs out of us and has to be suppressed. Shiva not only destroys the Universe but is also the destroyer of man's illusions, and the cycle of birth and death which binds us to this world.

Soon after the creation of this world, Shiva is believed to have appeared in the form of a pillar of fire, reaching into space at one end and into the bowels of the earth at the other, and neither Brahma nor Vishnu was able to trace the beginning or end of this supernatural manifestation. Therefore Shiva is symbolised as a Linga or Lingam (meaning a symbol) representing this endless pillar of cosmic power and light.

He is also worshipped as Lingodbhavamurti, in which the figure of Shiva emerges out of the pillar of fire, with Brahma and Vishnu standing on either side.

47
Nandi, the vehicle of Shiva

In all Shiva temples, his vehicle, Nandi the bull, faces the figure of Shiva symbolising the soul of man, the Jiva, yearning for Paramatma, the Great Soul (God).

48
Brahma and Vishnu witness Shiva emerging
from the Shiva Lingam, the cosmic pillar of
fire

49
Shiva as Lingodbhavamurti (emerging from
the Shiva Lingam)
Patteshwaram, Tamil Nadu

45

Cosmic Energy in its dynamic form is symbolised for us ordinary mortals in the form of Shakti, the World Mother, who is the power and energy by which the Great God creates, preserves and destroys the world. She is shown in many forms. As Uma or Parvati, she is the gentle consort of Shiva. As Kamakshi or Rajarajeshwari, she is the Great Mother. In one hand she holds a noose, signifying worldly attachments from which we should free ourselves. The hook in her other hand is indicative of her prodding us on to the path of righteousness. The sugarcane plant she carries is a symbol of the sweetness of the Mind. The arrows she holds in one hand are our five sense-perceptions which we have to conquer. In the form of Durga she rides the tiger, the ego and arrogance that Man has to subdue. With the weapons in her hand she fights the eight evils (hate, greed, passion, vanity, contempt of others, envy, jealousy and the illusions with which man binds himself). In her angry form she is known as Kali, the personification of Time. In this frightening form she destroys Mahishasura (the demon buffalo) who is the symbol of ignorance which is man's greatest enemy. Her arms and weapons are constantly flaying and fighting evil in all forms. The skulls she wears tell you that Man is mortal. Her dark form is symbolic of the future which is beyond our knowledge, and as Kali she tells you that Time (Kala) is immutable and all-powerful in the Universe.

50
Durga on her vehicle, the tiger

52
Parvati, Consort of Shiva
Thanjavur Art Gallery

Ganesha, also known as Ganapati or Vinayaka, is the son of Shiva and Parvati and is the first deity to be worshipped during any ritual, as he is considered the remover of obstacles. His huge body represents the Cosmos or Universe and his trunk the Pranava or OM, the symbol of the Brahman. His elephant's head denotes superior intelligence and the snake around his waist represents cosmic energy. The noose is to remind us that wordly attachments are a noose and the hook in his hand is to prod Man on to the path of righteousness. The rosary beads are for the pursuit of prayer and the broken tusk is symbolic of knowledge as it is with this tusk that he is believed to have acted as the scribe who wrote down the Mahabharata as dictated by Sage Vyasa. The *modaka* or sweet in his hand is to remind us of the sweetness of one's inner self.

The physical form of Ganesha is corpulent and awkward to teach us that beauty of the outward form has no connection with inner beauty or spiritual perfection. Ganesha, on his vehicle, the mouse, symbolises the equal importance of the biggest and the smallest of creatures to the Great God.

The other son of Shiva, Kartikeya, is also known as Kumara, Skanda, Subramanya, Shanmukha or Muruga (the last name used in Tamil Nadu). As Kartikeya he is designated the deity of war, guarding right and destroying evil. As Shanmukha, the six-headed, he teaches that we have five senses and the mind, and only when all six are in harmony is there spiritual growth. As Subramanya, he has two consorts, Valli and Devasena, who embody Jnana Shakti, the power of knowledge and Kriya Shakti, the power of action. He rides the peacock, reminding us not to let pride and egotism get the better of us. In his hand he holds the *vel* or sharp spear, symbolising the developed sharp intellect, and with it he guards the spiritual progress of the world.

53
Shiva, Parvati with their son, Skanda
Thanjavur, Tamil Nadu

48

54
Ganesha, the remover of obstacles

55
Shanmukha, the six-faced form of Kartikeya
Thanjavur, Tamil Nadu

56
Sage Vyasa dictating the Mahabharata to
Ganesha

49

Kartikeya and his vehicle, the peacock

Most visitors to our country wonder why gods and goddesses of the Hindu Pantheon are shown with several arms, and sometimes with several faces. The main reason is to show them to be supernatural, just as in some religions angels are shown to have wings. We are aware that the Supreme Brahman is formless. It is Man, in the primitive stages of society, who has given the Great Spirit understandable human forms of His power and His attributes, to teach the ordinary people of His greatness, His omniscience and His omnipotence.

Also, one must realise that Hinduism adopted and assimilated the religious beliefs of all the primitive tribes and peoples with whom the early Hindus came into contact. Its tolerance of all religions is unique as it did not destroy the beliefs of the peoples the ancient Hindus conquered but absorbed them. Every religion which Hinduism absorbed had its own gods and beliefs (some even had totems), and every race its own rituals and rites. Hinduism assimilated them all, never destroying the beliefs in the gods or the totems of any of the tribes and peoples whom the early Hindus conquered. It is one of the greatest miracles of the spiritual world that Hinduism gathered so many, many different religions in its fold, and brought thousands of differing religious beliefs under the umbrella of Vedic Hinduism, with the Upanishadic aphorism, *'Ekam Sat viprah bahudha vadanti'* (the Great God is One, and the learned only call Him by different names).

By the time Adi Shankara, the great Indian philosopher, arrived on the scene, there were thousands of gods and goddesses of the various races and tribes and innumerable and confusing rituals being performed by Hindus.

Born in Kalady in Kerala in the 8th century, Shankara was the greatest exponent of the Advaita philosophy (according to which God is within Man, and the Atma, the individual soul and the Brahman, the Universal Soul are one and not two). He refuted the Buddhist teaching that the world is totally unreal and said that the objective world does exist in relation to the ordinary mind but is not the Ultimate Reality. In relation to the latter, however, it is an illusion.

Travelling by foot several times to all corners of this vast land, in his short span of life of 32 years he established the earliest Hindu monastic order with Matams or Ashrams in the south, west, north and east of this country. (Even today we have Matams of this order at Sringeri and Kanchi in the south, Dwarka in the west, Badri in the Himalayas, and Puri in the east.) Each Matam was placed under an Acharya or teacher, called a Shankaracharya during his tenure, who propagated Advaita or the philosophy of Monism.

As a religious reformer in a period of spiritual crisis, as existed then (and exists now), he taught that *vijnana* (intuition), *vichara* (enquiry), and *anubhava* (experience), each have their place in spiritual experience but it is essential for knowledge to be acquired by personal investigation and one's own experience alone, as even the Vedas, he said, only reveal, they do not command. He postulated that all paths to God are ancillary to Jnana Marga or the path of knowledge.

He was one of the great mystical seers who, with their intuitory knowledge, anticipated many of today's scientific theories on primal energy (Shakti), the atom (Anu), vibrations of the Universe (Shabda Brahmam), and the physical and psychic world around us.

He also wrote commentaries on Vedanta, the Gita and the Upanishads, and gave new dimensions to devotional literature by including in it mysticism clothed in exquisite poetry.

Never forgetting the needs of the untutored devout of heart, he established new systems of worship for their guidance. He codified popular Hinduism and grouped all the gods and goddesses under six main streams of worship.

They are Shaiva (worship of Shiva), Vaishnava (worship of Vishnu), Shakta (worship of Shakti, the Mother Goddess), Saura (worship of Surya, the Sun God), Ganapatya (worship of Ganesha or Ganapati), and Kaumara (worship of Kumara, also known as Muruga or Subramanya). He taught that these six Bhakti-darshanas or paths of prayer are not in conflict but are for the choice of the worshipper striving to reach God.

Adi Shankara is therefore called the 'Shanmata-sthhapana—Acharya', the teacher who established the six-fold form of worship and taught that worship of any one of the deities was as good as worship of the other, reaching towards a common goal. He did not destroy any existing beliefs but brought order into the Hindu fold in a form which did not exist earlier. Many Hindu communities which had given up the path of Hindu beliefs came back to it, attracted by Shankara's intellectual approach to popular religion.

From this it must not be presumed that the aim of the Hindu is only to worship one of these six deities. Such worship is only the means to an end. The ultimate goal is for the individual soul in each one of us, known as the Atma, to attain the Brahman or the Universal Soul.

58
Surya, the Sun-God, in his chariot driven by seven horses
Kashipur, U.P.

59
Goddess Lakshmi emerges.
Amrita Manthana, the churning of the ocean
by the Devas and Asuras
Karnataka painting

53

Samsara

All souls are not able to achieve this happy state even after death. On the other hand most of us die only to be born again and again. This cycle of birth, death and rebirth is called Samsara, and every soul must go through this cycle of births and deaths before it attains *moksha* or liberation. Only the soul which reaches perfection in this life becomes one with the Brahman and is not born again.

Hindus believe in Samsara as we do not accept that the Great God would be cruel enough to create the great inequalities that exist in the world. He would not create one child beloved of happy parents, another who is handicapped or blind and a third who is unwanted, born to impoverished parents and left hungry. The inequalities of life are understandable only when we realise that they are of Man's own Karma or actions and not of God's creation. Each one of us at birth is the result of our past life. Our birth in this life is determined by the good and bad thoughts, words and deeds of a previous birth. This doctrine of *samsara* or rebirth is also called the theory of reincarnation or the transmigration of the soul and is a basic tenet of Hinduism. The Upanishads compare the passage of the soul to a caterpillar which climbs a blade of grass, leaves it and jumps on to a new one. Just as a man changes worn-out garments and wears new ones, so does the soul cast away one body and take on another.

However, we do not carry the burden of our previous lives in our consciousness, though we do in our sub-conscious minds. The birth of a musical genius in an unmusical family, or of great scholars and artistes whose education and environment do not explain their achievements, are a few evidences of the spill-over from previous births.

There are many such cases. One worth mentioning is of a young man who was a waster who could not even complete school. Suddenly one morning he was transformed into an erudite and knowledgeable mystic, and became a Sanyasi. His refined manners, wisdom and knowledge of the scriptures (without study or training) acquired overnight as it were, had no connection with his earlier life. It was as if, all of a sudden, some door in his inner being had been unlocked from a previous birth and illuminated his mind.

Karma

One of the basic beliefs of Hinduism is the law of Karma or Action, the law of cause and effect. It is explained by the saying, 'As we sow, so shall we reap.' A farmer cannot leave his fields fallow and expect a crop of wheat. Nor can he sow wheat and expect a field of rice. Similarly every good thought, word or deed begets a similar reaction which affects our next lives and every unkind thought, harsh word and evil deed comes back to harm us in this life or the next.

Often Indians are called fatalists on the grounds that it is the law of Karma that makes us accept Fate and not fight

60
The Mahabharata war
Thanjavur painting

misfortune. This is not so as Karma is far from being a fatalistic doctrine.

There are three stages of Karma. The only Karma that is beyond our control is Prarabdha Karma. According to this, the body or tenement the soul chooses to be born in is not under human control. The choice of parents, the environment of the home, and the physical condition of the new-born are the result of the sum total of favourable and unfavourable acts performed in a previous life. These cannot be changed. They are predetermined by the quality of the previous life. So also the time of death. Our scriptures aver that even a thousand spears will not kill you if your time on earth is not yet over, but when your end is near, even a blade of *kusa* grass could bring about your end. When each one of us has finished enjoying the good and paying for the bad deeds of the previous life, the time on earth is over. The soul leaves this body and goes into another to work out its destiny afresh, arising out of the good and bad deeds of this life.

The second stage is that of Samchita Karma which is the accumulated Karma of all our previous births which gives us our characteristics, tendencies, aptitudes and interests. This is why two children born of the same parents and given the same environment, for example, turn out to be very different in their capabilities and characteristics.

Samchita Karma is, however, changeable. With wisdom a man can change himself, improve his habits and get rid of evil thoughts and desires. Similarly one born with good characteristics could descend to a life of evil, setting aside his naturally good inclinations. Samchita Karma is therefore alterable by Man himself.

The third, Agami Karma, consists of the actions in our present life which determine our future in the later years of this life and in the next. It is entirely within our hands and our own free will. Man cannot change his past or birth, but he can mould his future. By evil thoughts, words or deeds, we mar our days to come. By purity of thought, compassionate words and deeds, righteous action without thought of the fruits thereof, we pave the way for a better life for all our tomorrows in this birth and the next.

Therefore Karma is not a fatalistic doctrine. It is a logical theory which explains differences in our births and temperaments and guides us in moulding our future lives.

Dharma

The aim of the Hindu being to break this chain of birth and rebirth that binds him to the earth, the first step to be taken on this path is for each one to perform well his own *dharma* or righteous duties. Hinduism is unique because it differentiates between the duties of man and man, as also between the duties to be followed at various stages of one's life. Lord Rama's *dharma* as an exile for 14 years was different to his later *dharma* as a ruler. The teacher, the nurse, the priest, a mother or father each has to follow his or her own *dharma*. Duties, whatever they are, have to be performed with excellence and moral purity as the goal.

The concept of Dharma is fundamental to Hinduism, as it is believed that it is only through the pursuit of Dharma that there is social harmony and peace in the world. The pursuit of Adharma (a path that rejects righteousness) leads to conflicts, discord and imbalance.

The saying, *'Dharanat Dharmah'* means Dharma sustains the world and it is that which holds the world together. It is duty performed with righteousness, with discipline and moral and spiritual excellence. Varnashrama Dharma is fundamental to Hindu belief and includes the duties of the various occupations, orders and classes *(varna)* and the duties in the four stages *(ashramas)* of one's life. It enjoins that each person's *dharma* or duty depends on his occupation, position, moral and spiritual development, age and marital status.

The Caste System

Although the caste system has now been legally abolished, it is interesting to know its origin. The original meaning of the word *'varna'* was order or class of people. When the Indo-Aryans invaded the country, they came across the local inhabitants whom they called Dasas or Dasyus. Instead of destroying them after conquest, as has happened in other civilisations, they absorbed them by giving them a lower but definite place in their society.

In time this system came to be four-tiered, with four classes, the Brahmanas or Brahmins (not to be confused with the Brahman) who were the teachers and priests, the Kshatriyas or warriors and rulers, the Vaishyas, those who followed commercial occupations, and the Sudras who performed manual labour and were also farmers and agriculturists. The word *'varna'* therefore implied the social order and not caste, as even Manu has given the difference between *varna* (class or order) and *jati* (sect of birth or caste). A man's *varna* depended as much on his mental and physical equipment as on heritage. Therefore it was a fluid state. A Brahmin for example, was one who evolved with the *guna* or qualities and performed the *karma,* or action, enjoined on a Brahmin. (It was only later that the word *'varna'* came to mean colour.)

The *jatis* (or sects) in time became more important than the four main classes. These were mainly occupational (like the goldsmith *jati,* the weaver *jati,* the carpenter *jati* etc.) and served the purpose of guilds which protected the interests of their members, trained the young and saw to it that no outsider entered the fold. In time these *jatis* or sects grouped themselves under the main classes which is why we speak today of four castes. However, it is not the caste of a man but his sect that is important to this day. Even today these sects often do not permit fluidity of movement, even where the old occupations have broken down and new ones have come in.

The untouchables or outcastes were originally those who had broken certain caste rules. For example, the Nayadis, who were considered outcastes of the lowest order, were originally Brahmins who were excommunicated for some reason. Also later the Hindus, who were originally meat-eaters, slowly changed their eating habits to vegetarianism, especially the Brahmins and Vaishyas who were influenced by early Buddhism and Jainism. With this change, those who ate beef or the meat of certain proscribed animals came to be considered outcastes or untouchables, as, by this time, the cow had come to be regarded akin to a mother, the people, being largely rural, having to depend on the cow's products for sustenance. (This is why the cow is given the reverence due to a mother in Hindu society to this day.)

However there is no religious sanction whatsoever in Hinduism to the concept of untouchability although later additions on the subject were inserted into the earlier scriptures to justify its existence. It was a purely social practice introduced by the upper castes to provide themselves with menial labour to perform certain tasks repulsive to themselves such as those of cemetery keepers, scavengers and cleaners. Hindu society has much to answer for this inhuman treatment of a whole section of its own people, but the Hindu religion had nothing to do with it.

These four classes were not as rigid in ancient times as they became later. In the Upanishads is the story of Satyakama, son of a servant maid, Jabala, who did not know his *gotra* or clan of origin as even his mother did not know who his father was nor his caste. He went to a great teacher known for his wisdom who took young Brahmin boys as disciples, and told him the truth of his parentage. He gave his name as Satyakama Jabala, after his mother. The Guru, impressed with the truthfulness of the young man, initiated him as a Brahmachari or student under him. He then gave him 400 head of cattle and asked him to take them to the forest and to return only when these became a thousand in number.

While living in the forest alone for years, Satyakama learnt of the Brahman, the Absolute, from communing with Nature, from the clouds in the skies, from the music of the birds, from the trees and the flowers and from the beauty of all Creation around and about him.

After he had 1000 head of cattle he returned. When his Guru gazed at the brilliant, shining face of his pupil, he knew that the young man had realised the Brahman and had only to complete this knowledge by study with his teacher. Although only Brahmins were initiated into higher religious education, not birth alone but aptitude also permitted the upward movement of the castes in Upanishadic times, as seen by the beautiful story of Satyakama Jabala.

The great Brahmin Rishi, Vyasa, was born when Parashara, the grandson of the Rishi Vasishta, fell in love with a beautiful dark-skinned woman of the fisher tribe, later named Satyavati. The child born to them was named Krishna Dvaipayana, after

61
Satyakama Jabala, in search of a guru

58

his dark colour *(krishna)* taken after his mother, and the island *(dvipa)* on which he was born. Only later did he become known as Veda Vyasa. Yet his knowledge of the Vedas determined his caste as a Brahmin Rishi and not his birth to a fisherwoman of a low caste. Vyasa is often worshipped as divinity in human form, so great is the regard given to him by Hindus through the ages. His birth to a tribal fisherwoman was not looked down upon, nor did it affect his position as a Brahmin sage of the highest caste.

(Similarly Valmiki, the author of the epic, the Ramayana, was a hunter of the lowest caste who came to be considered a Brahmin Rishi by virtue of his erudition.)

Satyavati subsequently married Santanu, King of Hastinapura. Her son Vichitravirya could not bear any children and her step-son, Bhishma, would not do so in view of a promise given to his late father not to marry or bear children, so that Satyavati's progeny would rule the kingdom.

According to the Niyoga custom of the times, on the death of a childless man or even if he were alive but could not father children, his brother could father children on his behalf. When it was found that her sons could not bear children, the great queen, Satyavati, called on the son born to her through Sage Parashara, the Sage Vyasa, and asked him to father children by her two daughters-in-law, which he did. A servant woman of the palace approached Vyasa in a spirit of great devotion and to her was born Vidura considered again one of the greatest of Brahmin sages (in view of his wisdom and knowledge of the Dharma Shastras) in spite of his mother being a servant woman of the lowest caste.

It was from the sons of Vyasa that the Pandavas and the Kauravas were descended. Their great-grandmother, Satyavati, belonged to a fisher tribe and their great-grandfather, Parashara, was a Brahmin sage. Yet because they were princes of the royal house of Hastinapura, they were considered Kshatriyas. In actual fact they were not so by birth, only by occupation, once again proving that caste was purely occupational.

Utanga, a childhood Brahmin friend of Krishna, took a boon from him that, in his wanderings, Krishna would provide him with water whenever he needed it. Once, when he felt very thirsty, he thought of the Lord and suddenly a Nishada (an outcaste hunter) appeared before him clothed in filthy rags, and offered water from his animal-skin water-bag. Utanga refused it and berated Krishna in his mind, as he felt he had not kept to his promise. The Nishada tried to persuade Utanga again and again to drink the water but Utanga was adamant. The hunter then disappeared and the Lord appeared before Utanga and told him that he had sent Indra, King of the Devas, as a hunter with *amrita,* the nectar of immortality. Since Utanga had not shown any wisdom but had continued to differentiate between man and man based on externals such as caste, he had missed the rare chance of attaining immortality. The moral of this story is obvious.

The disciples of the great philosopher, Adi Shankara, once asked a Chandala (an outcaste), to move away from his path. "Who are you and who am I? Is the Self within me different from yours?", queried the Chandala (believed to be Shiva in disguise). Shankara, realising the wisdom of these words, prostrated before the Chandala saying, "One who is established in the Brahman, be he a low-born Chandala or a twice-born Brahmin, verily I declare him my Guru".

As late as in the 8th century, an untouchable could be considered a Guru by one born a brahmin like Adi Shankara.

Status of Women

The status of women also in early Hindu society was an enviable one. Women so inclined could avail of the highest learning and there were many seers and philosophers like Maitreyi, Gargi, Vishavara, Ghosha and Apala. Adi Shankara, in a theological debate with Mandanamishra, appointed as judge the latter's wife Sarasavani, in view of her superior erudition and spiritual attainments. Warrior queens like Kaikeyi helped their husbands on the battlefield.

In princely families, the custom of *swayamvara* or selection of the groom by the princess garlanding the one of her choice amongst all the princes present, was the accepted norm. Inter-marriages were common and women often chose their own husbands. Shakuntala, the daughter of a Brahmin sage, chose Dushyanta, a Kshatriya prince, and married him. Santanu, a Kshatriya king, married Satyavati, a fisher-woman, who was crowned queen. Even after her husband's death she was revered as the Queen Mother, and decided many matters of state and problems of family successions.

Polygamy existed in some societies but mostly amongst princes who contracted several marriages with daughters of neighbouring rulers for political reasons. Polyandry was also practised in some areas. The classic example is Draupadi, who married the five Pandava brothers.

Girls were normally not married till they were in their late teens, sometimes even later. Hindu society as established by the Indo-Aryans was patriarchal, but many matriarchal societies of the Dravidian and the pre-Dravidian south continued to exist until quite late in history even after the adoption of Vedic Hinduism. (Today only Kerala in the south is matriarchal though even here changes are creeping in.)

The upper castes even earlier had tried to prevent (though unsuccessfully) inter-caste marriages as also the upward movement of the lower castes. Towards this end the Brahmins, for example, tried to make knowledge of the scriptures their monopoly and the rituals more and more elaborate so that they alone could interpret them. The Kshatriyas similarly tried to make rulership their birth-right and the Vaishyas attempted to become the only custodians of the wealth of the land.

However, it was only with the foreign invasions of the 11th century A.D. and later, starting with the raids of Mahmud of Ghazni and the Goris, that the caste system became rigid.

Unlike the Moghul rulers of a later period who were more tolerant in their treatment of the local people, the earlier invaders looted, plundered and destroyed temples, and marauding soldiers abducted young girls and women. As life, property and the chastity of women were of little value to the invaders, each community built a fortress of social norms around itself to protect its women. Many later-day social evils of the Hindus such as the rigid caste system, guarding the *sanctum sanctorum* in temples from entry except by the few (to prevent looting and plunder), child marriages (before a girl could be of an age attractive enough to be abducted), the shaving of widows' heads (to make them unattractive to the foreign soldier), the widespread practice of Sati (the burning of a widow with her dead husband), became the norms during this unsettled period of Indian history.

Hindu women lost their independence and became objects requiring male protection. In the process they also lost the opportunities they had earlier of acquiring knowledge and learning.

Hindu Reform

With the coming of British rule in India and the introduction of Western thought, there arose in India a new upsurge of intellectual searching and a re-evaluation of our ancient past. Hindu thinkers reassessed their weaknesses and traced them to the evils of the rigid caste system and to the social evils that had befallen women and the so-called untouchable castes. Starting from the early 19th century, several Indian reformers sprang up all over India and spread their message for purifying Hinduism of its excessive rites, rituals and orthodoxy and for abolishing the inequalities heaped on women in the name of the religion. To mention a few whose work led to reforms on a national scale, the earliest was Raja Rammohan Roy of Bengal. He preached against rituals and worked for the abolition of Sati. Although Sati means pure and chaste, the word had (in the last few centuries) been used to connote the immolation of a widow with her husband.

62
Swami Vivekananda

Another illustrious son of Bengal, Ishwar Chandra Vidyasagar popularised Sanskrit teaching amongst all castes and fought for widow remarriage.

The Prarthana Samaj was set up in Bombay for fighting the caste system and its great leaders were R. G. Bhandarkar, the famous Sanskrit scholar, and M. G. Ranade.

The greatest of them all, Swami Vivekananda, set up the Ramakrishna Mission, an organisation of service and social reform, and spread the message of true Hinduism throughout India and the Western world. He fought hard against orthodoxy and preached spiritual freedom, fearlessness and

63
Swami Dayananda Saraswati

the universalism of all religions, all of which were basic to Hindu spiritual beliefs.

Swami Dayanand Saraswati, a Gujarati Brahmin, fought against Hindu priesthood and wanted Hinduism to go back to its Vedic glory. He founded the Arya Samaj in 1875, a movement which was reformist, and attempted to unify the Hindus under the umbrella of Vedic Hinduism, shorn of later-day superstitions.

Annie Besant, Irish by birth, came to India in 1895 as a theosophist and worked for Hindu religious revival. Her admiration for Hindu thought gave great self-respect to Hindus at a time when they were looked down upon by their British rulers. She set up the Central Hindu College at Banaras which later became the nucleus of the Banaras Hindu University.

Mahatma Gandhi, the father of Independent India, made women take part in the freedom movement, and by this great act of vision, got rid of many of the social inequalities heaped on women. He also made the abolition of untouchability an integral part of the freedom movement. By not permitting untouchable Hindus in places of worship, Hindu society had been weakened, as the scriptures reiterated the equality of all men in the eyes of God. Many aspects of Gandhiji's national movement simultaneously also worked towards Hindu religious reform.

A great religious reformer who worked against untouchability was Narayana Guru of Kerala who not only fought against casteism but was also responsible for the high level of education and religious instruction of the lowest castes in that region.

Dr. C. P. Ramaswami Aiyar had fought all his life against orthodoxy and untouchability. In 1936, when he was Dewan of Travancore, the Maharaja's proclamation opened the temples of the state to all Hindus. For the first time in India, untouchables were allowed to enter places of worship. Mahatma Gandhi called this step 'the glory of a miracle,' especially as some of the worst aspects of casteism were practised in Kerala. Even Swami Vivekananda had bitterly spoken earlier of the "don't touchism" that prevailed there in the name of religion. From then on, several temples in other parts of India followed suit.

Each region in India threw up religious reformers, poets and saints, all of whom taught that social and religious reform had to go hand in hand. As a result, in 1950, Independent India laid down in the Constitution that untouchability could not be practised in any form. Also, the Constitution guaranteed full equality to all men and women. The Hindu Succession Act of 1956 made daughters equal heirs with sons.

Old habits however die hard and laws by themselves are not enough. The hearts of the people must change which will only happen when the upper castes understand the origin of the caste system, the fact of the fluidity of castes in ancient times,

the inter-mixing of castes within each one of us, and the
reasons for the later-day rigidity of the caste system.

The Four Stages of Life

Just as each caste had its particular duties to follow, there is
also the *dharma* of the four *ashramas* (or stages) in each of
our lives.

Brahmachari or Student

The first stage is that of the Brahmachari or the stage of life of
the student which began, in the case of the first three classes
which educated their children, with the Upanayana or the
thread ceremony. In ancient times girls were also given this
initiation, as can be seen from temple sculptures where women
also wear the sacred thread, but this was given up later on.

64
In meditation

The three threads remind a young man of the Pranava
(OM, the symbol of the Absolute), Medha (intelligence) and
Shraddha (diligence), the three essential guides for education.
He is taught the powerful Gayatri Mantra for the worship of
the Sun so that he may absorb its brilliance and effulgence.
In olden days students lived with their teacher or Guru in a
gurukula (or school) usually set in the midst of a forest.
The rich and the poor boy, the prince and the pauper, lived and
studied together. It was a life involving service to the Guru and
his family, the practice of Yoga, the study of the scriptures, the
arts and the sciences, and a life of simplicity, celibacy and
spartan self-discipline.

On their departure after the training was over, the Guru
exhorted his pupils to speak only the truth, to work without
forgetting Dharma, to serve elders, to remember the teachings
of the Vedas and to regard one's mother, father, teacher and
guest as divine beings to be revered and honoured.

65
In a gurukula

The beauty of the life of the student in the *gurukula* has few
parallels and the fall in the quality of education in schools and
colleges today can be traced to the inadequate emphasis placed
by present-day society on the totality of education and the need
for it to encompass all aspects of a student's life and not book
study alone. Equally serious today is the neglect of the study of
our past leading to rootlessness amongst the young.

Also, it is essential today that we reintroduce at least a
symbolic thread ceremony for all classes and sects of Hindus,
for boys and girls, and through it initiate the young into their
quest for knowledge.

Grihastha or Householder

The second stage in one's life is that of the Grihastha or householder. This stage begins when the student returns from his studies, marries and takes on the duties of a householder.

The Hindu marriage is a sacred step in one's spiritual growth, and not a contract. Like Goddess Parvati, the wife is *ardhangini,* part of her husband. No religious ritual can be performed by a man without his wife. No man's or woman's life is believed to be complete without marriage.

Every step taken in the marriage ceremony is symbolic.

The wedding ceremony takes place in front of Agni, the god of Fire. Agni personifies the power and light of the Great God. On one side of the fire is a pot of water for purification, and on the other, a flat stone.

At the start of the marriage ceremony, the father of the bride gives away his daughter, symbolic of Goddess Lakshmi, to the groom, who is deemed to be Vishnu himself. The *mantra* that is chanted is the same that was first recited by King Janaka while giving his daughter, Seeta, in marriage to Rama:

"This Seeta, my daughter, will be your helpmate in discharging your religious obligations. Take her hand in yours and make her your own. She will be your alter ego, ever devoted to you. She is blessed and will be as inseparable from you as is your shadow".

Then comes the *panigrahana* ceremony. Holding the bride's hand in his, the groom says, "I hold your hand for happiness. May we both live to a ripe old age. You are the queen and shall rule over my home. You are the Sama Veda, I am the Rig Veda", (implying that they are part of one another). "I am heaven and you are the earth. Let us marry and be joined together." The couple go around the fire and water thrice, clock-wise, while the groom says these words.

They then touch each other's hearts while the groom says, "Your heart I take in mine. Whatever is in your heart shall be in mine, whatever is in mine shall be in yours. Our hearts shall be one, our minds shall be one. May God make us one". The bride then mounts the stone, symbolic of the strength of their union.

The couple then take the *saptapadi* or seven steps together during which the groom prays, "With the first step for food and sustenance, with the second step for strength, with the third step for keeping ours vows and ideals, with the fourth step for a comfortable life, with the fifth step for the welfare of our cattle, with the sixth step for our life together through all the seasons, and with the seventh step for fulfilling our religious duties". Walking hand in hand, taking seven steps together is symbolic of their lives together as man and wife and, equally, as close friends.

The bride prays to Agni, the god of Fire, to witness the marriage, for the prosperity of her new home. Water is sipped by the couple to wash away impurities and to start a new life.

On the wedding night, the groom is shown Dhruva (the Pole Star), and asked to be as unmoving and constant in his love and devotion as the child Dhruva was to Vishnu (for which he was turned into the unmoving Pole Star after death). The bride is shown the stars, Vasishta and Arundati (part of the Great Bear constellation, known as the Sapta Rishis or seven sages in Indian astronomy), symbolic of a devoted couple who are never separated and are always seen together in the skies.

All other customs, such as tying the *mangalasutra* or *thali*, putting *sindoor* on the parting, and exchanging garlands are purely local social customs and not instrinsic or essential to the marriage ceremony. The existence of *agni* (fire) and taking the seven steps are basic essentials of a Hindu wedding.

The marriage ceremony, if performed with faith, is considered of great spiritual merit to the parents of the bride who give away their precious daughter.

The word *'vivaha'* meaning marriage also means that which sustains Dharma or righteousness. It is realised that to make a marriage successful is difficult and requires great sacrifices and adjustability which also help develop character.

It is the householder who practises right conduct (Dharma), earns material wealth (Artha), permits himself a life of love and passion (Kama) with his wife and attains salvation (Moksha).

Therefore the second stage, the *ashrama* of the Grihastha, is considered the most important of the four. The householder is expected to earn a living with integrity and by honest means and to give away one-tenth of what he earns in charity.

He is expected to give happiness and joy to his wife by providing her with a good home. It is obligatory for him to look after his children, educate and marry them.

Charity is essential in a married couple's life. Food is to be given to crows and birds, to cattle and other animals everyday. Hospitality and providing for one's guests are the main duties of a married couple who should not eat their main meal for the day without feeding a guest, a visitor, a relative or a poor man.

The Grihastha's life is full of social and spiritual obligations which challenge his capabilities to the hilt and try him sorely. His trials and tribulations in this period, if faced without deviation from Dharma, enable him to evolve into a superior human being with harmony as the key-note of his success.

66
Yogi in meditation

Vanaprastha

Once one's grown-up children are settled and they are able to run their own lives and look after their young children, it is time for middle-aged couple to enter the third stage and to become Vanaprasthas or, literally, those who retire to the forest. In modern parlance this means that the time has come to detach oneself from the jungle of wordly desires and attachments, concentrate on philosophical study and retire to the sylvan peace of contemplation, meditation and spiritual pursuits.

Unfortunately, in today's world, few give up their wordly desires at any stage of their lives, so even the third stage is rarely reached as most people are still involved in the rat-race of making money and acquiring more and more consumer goods, each bigger and better than one's neighbour's.

At no time in the history of our land has this acquisitiveness reached the stage we are in today. Acquiring money by any means, fair or foul, aspiring for high positions, using money to gain political power, judging a man by his financial status in life, are some of the depths to which the Vanaprastha of today has fallen. These in turn have led to a widespread fall in values away from the Hindu ideal where the one most revered was not the king (with the wealth of the nation at his command) not the shopkeeper or merchant, but the mendicant and Sanyasi, who begged for alms even to feed himself.

Sanyasi

Out of those few who reach the Vanaprastha *ashrama,* barely a handful reach the fourth stage of the Sanyasa *ashrama.* One who takes to Sanyasa gives up all wants, has no needs, does not accept money, and renounces the world. He lives on alms or the fruits of the forest and spends his time in meditation. He is beyond the rules and regulations of ordinary living and is a *jivanmukta,* or one liberated from ordinary life. Unfortunately visitors to our country think that all orange clad men (called *sadhus* or peaceful men) are holy men or Sanyasis. A few are, but the majority are the "drop-outs" of Hindu society, often preying on the gullible.

Yoga

An evolved Sanyasi, however, is also usually a Yogi. The word Yoga means to yoke or unite, and it is used to imply the means or path by which the individual soul unites with God.

Yoga is today confused with physical exercises alone. Actually it includes eight types of disciplines.

The first two, *yama* and *niyama,* purify the heart and bring about ethical discipline. *Yama* means abstention of all types — abstention from killing, untruth, theft and possession of property. It also means the practice of celibacy. *Niyama* means observance of purity (both external and internal) and practice of austerities or *tapasya.* It includes supreme contentment, the

67
Ramalinga Swami

68
Ramakrishna Paramahamsa

69
Sharada Devi

66

study and knowledge of the scriptures and surrender to the Supreme God.

The next three, *asana, pranayama,* and *pratyahara* are preliminary steps to Yoga. *Asanas* are the Yogic postures which, when practised regularly, steady the mind for concentration and discipline the body. *Pranayama* are breathing exercises which improve the condition of the lungs, heart and nervous system, bring about good health and thereby give a tremendous sense of well-being. They also result in serenity and steadfastness of the mind without which Yoga is meaningless. *Pratyahara* means shutting out all outward impressions from the mind and looking inward.

The last three steps are called Raja Yoga and include *dharana, dhyana* and *samadhi. Dharana* means concentration on any one object which could be a light within the mind or a form or image of God used in prayer. Then comes *dhyana* or meditation involving an unceasing flow of thoughts and ideas towards this object. Such meditation leads to the final state known as *samadhi,* when the subject of the meditation and the object become one.

Samadhi itself involves two steps. The first is conscious *samadhi* when the Yogi attains supernatural powers by the strength of his Yogic practices, becomes clairvoyant, adept at mind-reading and thought-transmission. These powers, called *siddhis,* are looked down upon in Yoga, but unfortunately most Sanyasis never go past this stage. At the same time unevolved persons and the illiterate masses are completely taken in by such persons because they appear to perform miracles, promise to cure diseases and to bring material prosperity to those devoted to them. Such Sanyasis should be guarded against.

The Sanyasi who ignores such powers and progresses further attains the superconscious or *nirvikalpa samadhi* when the mind is in full union with God. The Yogi in this stage has broken the bonds of Samsara, the cycle of births and deaths and is verily a liberated soul.

From time immemorial great Yogis and Sanyasis have been Gurus (or teachers) who have taught the truths of the Hindu religion and spread its messages to the masses and to intellectuals, to guide them in matters of the spirit. Some of them have spread these truths all over the world.

Shri Ramalinga Swami, Shri Ramakrishna Paramahamsa, Sharada Devi, Swami Vivekananda, Swami Rama Tirtha, Shri Aurobindo, Shri Ramana Maharishi and Swami Sivananda are a few of the many great souls no longer with us whose spiritual messages, loud and clear, still guide mankind.

Hundreds of Hindu Yogis and Sanyasis are to be found all over the world today who work for the spiritual progress of our great land. Whereas there are quite a few who trade on the gullibility of the innocent, there are several genuinely great Gurus who teach those amongst us who are totally ignorant about our own religion and guide others towards the path of

70
Shri Aurobindo

spiritualism. To such Sanyasis and their work of spreading the truths of the Hindu Religion, we should bow in all humility.

Vices and Virtues

A common question asked is whether Hinduism believes in the sins of Man and the punishment of God being meted out to those committing these sins.

Hindus consider only self-centred desire as a sin which leads to all the evils of mankind. However we believe that it is not God who punishes us but our actions or Karma, as explained earlier.

There are, however, six main obstacles or vices which detract Man from performing his *dharma*. They are *kama* (lust), *krodha* (unjust and vicious anger), *lobha* (greed and avarice), *moha* (infatuation arising out of ignorance and delusion), *mada* (vanity resulting from egoism) and *matsarya* (envy and jealousy).

To overcome them one should practise some of the essential virtues which are taught to us in our various epics. They are *satyam* (truth), *ahimsa* (non-violence), *vairagya* (detachment from desires), purity of thought, word and deed, and self control.

Satyam does not only mean merely speaking the truth. It means the permeation of Truth in our thoughts, words and deeds and in our relationships with fellow human beings. Hinduism is itself based on Truth and the pursuit of Truth. Truth is beautiful and untruth ugly. The former leads to justice and righteousness in the world and to scientific progress. It blazes new trails in the spiritual progress of Man.

Truth must not be confused with morality. Truth is unchangeable. Concepts of morality change from time to time. Much earlier it was explained that Hinduism alone of all religions accepts that the laws of Man are changeable in each age. The Dharma of ancient India enjoined that the brother-in-law of childless widow should marry the widow so that she could bear children. Today this is no longer the practice. Punishments of thieves by cutting off their hands was a common practice in ancient times, but is no longer permitted. A man's *dharma* in ancient India followed his caste or sect. Today one born a Brahmin owns a leather factory, one born a Kshatriya takes to farming, one born a butcher becomes a Sanskrit scholar. The castes no longer follow their occupational divisions. Yet society and politicians misuse the defunct caste system for their own ends, the upper castes in order to maintain an artificial social status for themselves, and the lower castes, for getting special privileges for themselves.

Dharma or the laws of society therefore change from age to age and should not be confused with Truth which is unchangeable, transcending Time and Space. All the other virtues are only different aspects of Truth which is all-encompassing. Even the slightest deviation from Truth is considered Untruth and is unacceptable.

71
Ramana Maharishi

The belief *'Ahimsa paramo dharmah'*, or that Ahimsa or non-violence is the greatest of laws, is Hinduism's great contribution to mankind. Mahatma Gandhi made this the cornerstone of the Indian Independence movement, and oppressed people all over the world have adopted it or drawn hope from it.

Ahimsa is often confused with non-killing alone. A businessman may destroy his competitor by unfair means but be a vegetarian in his food habits. He thinks he is practising Ahimsa but he is not.

Vegetarianism is one of the goals of Ahimsa in its ultimate form, but it also means not hurting anyone or any being in thought, word or deed and not killing or causing pain to man or animal. On the positive side, Ahimsa implies kindness to all people and one's neighbours, care of animals and birds, indeed, of all life. It teaches hospitality of the highest order to be extended to friends and enemies.

72
Swami Sivananda

The reverence given to the cow, based on Ahimsa or not killing one who provides a largely vegetarian nation with milk products (much as a mother provides food for her young), is a part of our reverence for Ahimsa.

The reverence for plants and trees was ingrained in the people by asking them to protect the *vana-devata,* the heavenly beings which reside inside trees. Thus, by preventing the cutting down of trees, Hindus were the first to give spiritual emphasis to ecology and the environment, considered modern-day subjects.

Ahimsa is not a result of cowardice but of strength. It is only the very strong in spirit who can choose this path as, in today's world, with its napalm and neutron bombs, it is easy indeed to practise violence and very hard to desist from it and to practise Ahimsa.

The third important virtue, detachment, is not a virtue enjoined on the young. It is only at the stage of a Grihastha or householder that one should slowly start performing acts without attachment to the results. When he becomes a Vanaprastha, a man should detach himself from attachments to the body and soul and work for the good of all. Detachment does not mean not loving one's near and dear ones. It means extending love to all equally and not working only for or loving only the ones to whom we are attached by family or emotional bonds. The Upanishads so rightly say, *'Vasudhaiva Kutumbakam'* (the whole world is my family).

Purity is often misunderstood in India to be bodily purity alone. Rules of bathing, of eating and drinking, all emphasise the importance of purity, as personal cleanliness is considered a step towards godliness. But purity of the mind and spirit are equally important, as is civic cleanliness, and often forgotten in our obsession with physical purity.

The last virtue, that of self-control, implies control of the five senses, the mind and the spirit. The importance of discipline at

69

the stage of a Brahmachari, during studentship, first initiates the young into the control of the body and the mind and, in the later stages, as a Grihastha and a Vanaprastha, to the control of the spirit also. Self-control does not mean denying oneself. It means moderation in all things and avoidance of indulgence. Even loose talk and harmful gossip are to be avoided, as are over-eating and excessive drinking. Keeping one's body, mind and spirit under control is one of the virtues enjoined on the Hindu at every stage of his life.

We have gone through the main tenets of Hinduism, the concepts of Samsara, Karma and Dharma and the aim of the individual soul to be liberated from the cycle of births and deaths so as to reach the Brahman or the Absolute.

The Three Paths to the Brahman

To achieve this spiritual union with the Supreme Soul (Brahman), there are believed to be three main paths, Bhakti Yoga (through Bhakti or devotion), Karma Yoga (by Karma or action) and Jnana Yoga (the path of wisdom or spiritual enlightenment).

Bhakti Yoga

The most common of these three paths, which is chosen by the vast majority, is the path of Bhakti or devotional worship. In this the devotee chooses a form of the Saguna Brahman or Ishwara in any one of His manifestations and realises God through love and devotion. Intense faith in a personal deity, called the Ishta-Devata, is characteristic of Bhakti worship. The Ishta-Devata can be one of the Trinity, any one of the Avatars or any other deity of one's choice.

In the first stage of Bhakti Yoga, the form of the Ishta-Devata is visualised by means of an image or icon. It is installed in the home and *pooja* (ritual of personal worship) performed daily.

The rules for performing *Poojas* are given in the Agamas in great detail. The image or icon or even a picture of the deity is kept in a corner of the home facing eastwards, towards the rising sun. Everyday devotional worship is performed either simply or elaborately according to one's inclination. In its simple form, the worshipper sits in meditation in front of the icon.

In its more elaborate form, a daily *pooja* is performed.

Before settling down to perform *pooja*, the worshipper adorns the centre of his forehead with red powder *(kumkum)*. Also worn are sandalwood paste or holy ashes *(vibhuti)*. This spot between the brows is the seat of latent wisdom and of concentration of the mind, so vital for worship.

Women usually wear a red mark as red is the colour of auspiciousness as also of power. This mark is worn by girls and women all the time and by men nowadays only during worship. This is to remind us of the power of the three consorts of the Trinity and the grace they bestow on worshippers.

As it is a sign of auspiciousness, in former days (and even today in orthodox homes) it was not worn by widows or when there was death in the family. This is why it is mistakenly thought to be a sign of marriage in women. This is not so as even unmarried girls and men wear this mark. (In some parts of the country, however, *sindoor* or red powder is worn on the hair parting by married women only.)

Although the *kumkum* or *bindi* is usually worn as a round circular spot, women adorn their foreheads with different designs. A crescent moon reminiscent of the moon adorning Shiva's locks is drawn on the forehead by worshippers of Shiva, or a star to remind themselves of the great Universe.

Men who are devotees of Shiva wear *vibhuti* or holy ashes on the forehead in three horizontal lines to remind themselves of the three aspects of God-head, Creation, Preservation and Destruction. Also that the human body ends in ashes, as Hindus cremate the bodies of their dead, possibly one of the few peoples of the world to do so.

Women devotees of Vishnu wear the *tilak*, a straight line in red, though this custom is on the decline with young people. Men devotees wear a 'Y' or 'U' sign in white (with or without a red line in the centre) symbolising the sacred feet of Vishnu, the red line depicting Goddess Lakshmi, also known as Sree Devi.

In some parts of the country this 'U' sign is believed to symbolise the sacred lotus opening out at the feet of Lord Vishnu.

Devotees of Krishna wear a sandalwood 'U' mark as Krishna is the beloved of all and the fragrance of sandalwood is symbolic of the fragrance of his love for his devotees.

These marks on the forehead were mistakenly called caste-marks by the British and this appellation unfortunately continues. However, they are not caste-marks and at best they only point out if the wearer is a follower of the Shaiva or Vaishnava faith. Even here the demarcation exists only for men as all women wear the same red dot on the forehead. (Today young women treat this as a beauty mark and use powders of different colours matching their clothes.)

73
The ritual of pooja

The next step in *pooja* or devotional worship is the lighting of lamps before the image which symbolises the dispelling of ignorance and the illumination of the mind with knowledge.

Water is then sipped and sprinkled, suggesting purification of one's physical self and one's environment, before the act of worship. The next step is the offering of flowers which represents the *atma* or the soul of the worshipper being offered to God. Fruits and food cooked at home are ceremonially offered to the deity to thank God for the bounty bestowed by Him on the home. Coconut, betel leaves and other offerings call upon God to bless the home with children and happiness.

71

Incense is waved before the icon (symbolising the fragrance of God's love) and camphor is burnt (representing the destruction of our egos and arrogance). The burning of camphor and waving it clockwise before the deity is called *arti* and symbolises the surrender of the worshipper to the will of God. The ringing of tinkling bells during *arti* is to keep out other noises so that the worshipper can concentrate on prayer.

Circumambulation is now performed by walking around the image three times to show that, as God is the Universe, the worshipper crosses the three worlds, the nether regions, the earth and the heavens, to reach Him. All circumambulation is performed clockwise following the earth's movement around the Sun.

The figure "three" is important is Hinduism as it symbolises many things at different times. It represents the three aspects of the Great God — Brahma, Vishnu and Shiva. It represents the three worlds which are part of our Universe.

It also points out the three great aims of Hindu thought, Satyam, Shivam and Sundaram (meaning Truth, Auspiciousness and Beauty), depicted in the trident of Shiva. It reminds us of the three qualities *(gunas)* of Man, *sattwa* (purity and tranquillity), *rajas* (passion) and *tamas* (inertia).

Pooja is so much a part of daily living as laid down in each Agama that every Hindu knows which flower or leaf should be used for each deity. For example, the *tulasi* (*tulsi* or holy basil) is sacred to Lord Krishna as Tulasi was a great devotee of his and begged that she should always be near him ever after death. Krishna turned her into a plant and asked his worshippers to use *tulasi* leaves as part of worship to him so that his devotee's wishes could be fulfilled.

Similarly, the austere *bilva* leaves (bael leaves of the woodapple tree) are used in Shiva worship, white flowers (symbolising the purity of knowledge) for Saraswati, and red flowers (symbolising power) for the worship of Shakti or Parvati.

Fasts are undergone and feasts held on fixed days as part of worship. The eleventh day of the Full and New Moon, for example, are days of fasting as are the days of the birth of Rama and Krishna. (After the moment of birth, there is feasting and rejoicing.) Every month, practically, has days of fasting and feasting given in the Hindu calendar. The fruit and milk or other more spartan diets prescribed for days of fasts help to maintain good health.

The Agamas lay down details of the observances of festivals which are so many and so much a part of Hindu life, giving great joy to the ordinary people and lending colour to their otherwise drab lives.

Such rituals are the first step in Bhakti or devotional worship and are called Apara Bhakti. Pilgrimages, visits to temples, taking part in feasts and festivals are all part of this first stage.

It must however be understood that the image installed is not considered God, as is often misunderstood, but is considered a symbol (or *pratika*) of God-head. In order to get the devotee to concentrate his mind totally on God, such an image (or *pratima*) helps in the first and early stages of worship. The use of images in worship was not known in early Vedic times but only introduced in the later Puranic period, mainly for the worship of the masses.

Throughout, it may be noticed, only the words, 'image', 'deity' or 'icon', have been mentioned as the word 'idol' is often used to denigrate Hinduism and to give the title, 'idol-worshippers' to Hindus.

It must be clearly understood that Hindus do not worship the image or the figure but consider the icon as a symbol of God-head. When a soldier goes to war, he carries his country's flag with him which he reveres and protects with his life. The soldier does not think the flag to be his country but a symbol representing the country for which he is fighting.

Similarly the picture or icon is considered a symbol of God and is not, by any stretch of the imagination, thought to be God Himself, except in the wider sense that God is everywhere.

The image of Christ on a cross or of the Madonna and Child Jesus in a Catholic church are never called idols, as the word 'idol' is derogatory and the religious leaders of such organised religions would never permit such a word to be used, and very rightly so.

Yet the image which a Hindu devotee keeps in his prayer room or instals in a temple, as a symbol of man's aspirations towards the same Great God, was called an 'idol' by foreign missionaries and this description continues to this day. Insults are heaped on Hindu worship only because Hindus are a pacific people who tolerate derision of their religious practices.

Coming back to Bhakti Yoga, in this first stage of worship called Apara Bhakti, the devotee asks or prays for something in return. It could be a prayer for a worldly request such as prosperity, a prayer for help for one's near and dear ones, for mental peace, for consolation in sorrow or comfort in adversity. Hinduism accepts that the mental level of all persons is not the same and that, to the majority of the populace, such personalised worship and asking for favours is alone possible.

The higher stage, the next step in Bhakti, is called Para Bhakti, where the devotee is consumed with love for his Ishta-Devata. He sees Him everywhere and is intoxicated by his vision of Him to the exclusion of all else. His love is all-consuming. He performs no Poojas or rituals but dances with joy at the all-pervading ecstasy of his divine love. Such a devotee inspires others to follow his path, the path of pure bliss. In this stage of Bhakti, the devotee sees no other deity, believes in none else other than his Divine Beloved. He asks for no gifts from God, except to be always drowned in thoughts of Him. He sees God in everything and everywhere. He is mad in the eyes of the world but reaches divinity through Ekanta Bhakti or single-

minded love for Divinity in the form of his Ishta-Devata, who is one aspect or form of the Great God.

In this stage of Bhakti the devotee asks for nothing in return from God and loves Him for Himself. Such Bhakti elevates the devotee until, in the final stage, he becomes one with Divinity.

Bhakti or devotion, can itself be of many forms. In *santa bhava*, the devotee looks on God as his father, as in the love of the child Dhruva for Vishnu. In *sakhya bhava*, the devotee treats God as a close personal friend as in Arjuna's relationship with Krishna, or the boatman Guha's love for Rama. In *dasya bhava*, the devotee looks on God as his master as in the case of Hanuman and Rama. In *kanta bhava*, the devotee looks on God as her husband as in the case of Andal and Lord Vishnu. In *madhurya bhava*, the devotee looks on God as her beloved as in the attitude of the *gopis* (milkmaids) towards Krishna.

The Tamil poet, Subramanya Bharati, visualised Krishna as friend, mother, father, servant, king, disciple, *guru*, child, lover, husband and God in his poems. These several forms of Bhakti can be well understood if one attends a Bharata Natyam classical dance performance. In one dance, the danseuse takes on the role of a devotee, in another, that of the consort of the Lord and in a third, as one craving for the company of her Divine Lover.

Bhakti or devotion can be of any form or of many forms. Each devotee can worship and adore God in his own way. His adoration of God is as if a lotus of a thousand petals opens up in joy to greet the rising sun. The ecstatic joy of a pure Bhakta or devotee so moves people that even the knowledgeable ones fall at his feet and the ignorant are transported to the realms of wisdom.

Bhakti or devotion in its ultimate form binds the devotee to God without any restrictions of caste or colour, nor does it accept any rules of worship.

Sabari, the tribal woman, tasted each fruit on the tree and kept the best aside for Lord Rama who happily ate them when she offered the fruit already tasted by her.

Kannappa Nayanar, an unlettered hunter, brought the flesh of the animals he killed in the forest and offered it first to the Shiva Lingam which he worshipped with great devotion. He brought water in his mouth (as his hands were not free) and spat it on the Lingam as part of the purification ritual in worship. Yet his devotion and heart were so pure that he is considered one of the greatest of Bhaktas who became one with God.

Atma-nivedan or offering oneself to God, Prapatti and Sharanagati or total surrender to God, are the highest forms of Bhakti or devotion.

The abject surrender by such devotion also gives great lisence to the devotee to view the object of his devotion in any form appealing to him. Lord Krishna was a child of ten when Radha

74
Saint Thiruvalluvar

75
Shri Madhvacharya

and the *gopis*, seeing divinity in him, worshipped and adored him. Yet several great devotees of Krishna brought in *madhurya bhava*, the love of a woman for her beloved, in the love of Radha and the *gopis* for Krishna. The all-absorbing madness and love of the milkmaids of Brindavan who sang and danced in divine ecstasy, has often been reduced to physical love by poets and artists to whom the latter form is more understandable.

Great Bhaktas abound in every nook and corner of this land and are far too many to recount. Their devotion has resulted in drawing the masses to the path of worship and has effectively broken down the caste system as they themselves were of all castes, from the highest to the lowest. Bhakti or devotional worship teaches that all men are the same in the eyes of God, and only the quality of worship raises Man to the level of divinity.

Some of the earliest devotees or Bhaktas who influenced the people by their devotion were the 12 Alwars (Azhvars), of whom one, Andal, was a woman and the 63 Nayanmars (of whom three were women). They lived in the Tamil region between the 4th and the 9th centuries but their poetry and music resound in the hearts of the people to this day, as does the poetry of Thiruvalluvar going back to the 2nd century or even earlier.

The Bhakti movement received great impetus from the early medieval period onwards with the advent of foreign invasions which resulted in widespread destruction of temples and mass conversions which shook the Hindu faith.

The movement was spear-headed by Ramanuja followed by Madhvacharya and later by Vallabhacharya. The lights of this movement are legion but a few of the stars of the firmament can be mentioned. Nimbarka, Basava and Purandaradasa, Ramananda and Shankara Deva, Tulsidas and Narsi Mehta are household names in different parts of the country, and their messages, poetry and music are still with us.

Chaitanya of Bengal was intoxicated with Krishna and may be considered the forerunner of the Krishna worship which has spread all over the world today.

Maharashtra produced several saint devotees. Eknath, Dnyaneshwar, Namdev, Sant Tukaram, Samartha Ramdas, Gora Kumbhar, Chokha, Janabai and many others thrill the devoted with their poetry and music left for posterity.

Bhakta Meera of Rajasthan, of princely origin, totally surrendered herself to Krishna, and hungered for eternal union with him. Her songs vibrate in our hearts to this day.

Jayadeva, Kabir, Saint Thyagaraja, Shirdi Sai Baba and so many more fill our hearts with some of the divine ecstasy which was the hallmark of their lives.

76
Shri Vallabhacharya

77
Shri Basava

78

79

80

81

78
Bhakta Andal

79
Sant Tulsidas

80
Shri Krishna Chaitanya

81
Shri Narsi Mehta

82
Sant Dnyaneshwar

83
Sant Tukaram

84
Bhakta Meerabai

85
Saint Thyagaraja

86
Shri Purandaradasa

87
Sant Kabir

88
Sai Baba of Shirdi

82

83

84

85

86

87

88

There are nine types of *bhakti,* any of which can be chosen by a devotee as his path.

They are, *shravana* (listening to the glories of the Lord, hearing His names repeated), *keertana* (singing His praises, chanting His names), *smarana* (remembering Him, concentrating one's thoughts on Him), *paadasevana* (worshipping at His holy feet), *archana* (offering flowers while repeating His names), *vandana* (making obeisance to the Lord with respectful fervour), *daasya* (treating God as master), *sakhya* (or as a dear friend) and *atmanivedana* (complete surrender of one's self to the Lord).

Karma Yoga

The second path to God-head is through Karma Yoga or union with God through action. This path is chosen by the few men and women for whom selfless service in their professions is their chosen goal. Karma Yoga teaches that work for work's sake is the aim and not work for its rewards. Nishkama Karma or action without attachment to the fruits of one's action, is the highest goal of this path. Rigid self-discipline and self-restraint, total absorption in one's path of action, justice and compassion towards all, the placing of the highest norms of dedicated service upon oneself, are the ideals of Karma Yoga. A Karma Yogi is a person to whom no work is inferior, as action is his means of attaining God, and work is his form of worship.

Jnana Yoga

The third path, the most difficult, and therefore the one chosen by the very few, is Jnana Yoga or the path of knowledge or wisdom. It is not mere knowledge but spiritual enlightenment achieved through the intuitive intellect, in its sublime and evolved form.

At the first stage, the Jnani or the wise one equips himself with the tools required for his ascent, such as knowledge of the Vedas, the Upanishads, the Bhagavad Gita and other books of his choice.

He then practises *viveka* (discrimination and analysis), *vairagya* (detachment), *sama drishti* (when all beings are equal in his eyes) and equanimity (when neither worldly joys nor sorrows affect him).

In the next step he takes the help of a Guru (or teacher) who is well established in the Brahman, who can guide him in his doubts. He then reflects on what he has learnt and gets rid of the chaff from the grain. He finally practises deep meditation on the Absolute Brahman. At this stage his mind should be unmoving like the lighted wick of a lamp which does not sway but stands firm and steady.

In the Katha Upanishad is the story of Nachiketas, a young man who seeks Yama, the god of Death, to answer his doubts on life after death.

Yama explains to him the nature of the Brahman and says, "Arise, awake! Go to the best teachers and learn from them!

The path to the Brahman is as narrow and as difficult to traverse as a razor's edge. Yet great joy greets one who attains this supreme knowledge".

In Bhakti Yoga there is a distinction between God and His perfection and Man and his imperfections which has to be broken down. In Karma Yoga there is the difference between the ethical ideal of perfection in action and Man's inadequacies which he has to conquer. In Jnana Yoga, through the path of spiritual wisdom, the Jnana Yogi bridges the gap and becomes one with the Brahman. Hinduism is unique in that it accepts that oneness with the Brahman and Moksha or salvation can be achieved in this life itself and do not have to wait for a heaven after death.

The path of Jnana Yoga is considered by many to be superior to Bhakti Yoga. The great philosopher, Appayya Dikshitar, writes, "Lord, in my meditations I have attributed forms to Thee who art formless. In singing hymns of Thee, I have belied the truth that Thou art indescribable. By going on pilgrimages, I have denied Thy omnipresence. Forgive me these three-fold faults".

Hindu scriptures point out that rites and rituals and pilgrimages to holy places are not the aim of religion but only the first and lowest step. The second step is the worship of God through symbols such as images or icons. The third step is mental worship, by meditation, concentration and contemplation. The highest step is that of the Jnana Yogi, who, by spiritual enlightenment, has realised the Brahman, the Universal Spirit.

Hinduism believes that man's true conversion in the path of religion should be vertical, from the lower step to the highest, and not by a horizontal movement from one faith to another, as all religions have the same goal and none are superior or inferior. Few religions accept such a tolerant approach to the universalism of all religions.

Jnana Yoga has seemed the most acceptable path for intellectuals and for thinking people from time immemorial. However, the three great obstacles in this path towards spiritual enlightenment are *avidya,* Maya and the *upadhis.*

89
The illusion of the rope and the snake

Avidya means not only ignorance but also illusion. We go into a dark room, see a rope and think it is a snake. Similarly Man confuses his Jiva or soul with his body, senses and mind. This is *avidya* or ignorance arising out of Maya, which is the veil of illusion by which we think that the Brahman the Universal Soul, and the Jiva, or individual soul, are separate, and that the different souls in the world are separate from each other.

The *upadhis* are the sheaths which, like layers of an onion, enclose the individual soul. Of these the body and the vital breath constitute the physical body. The mind, the intellect, and the psyche form the psychic and the subtle body.

All these covering skins have to be transcended by Vidya (knowledge and insight) and by Jnana (wisdom). Then only can Nirvana or spiritual enlightenment be attained.

To guide the Jnana Yogi, our scriptures have given guidelines on the nature of the Brahman, the Universal Soul. Some of the well-known sayings are:

Sarvam Khalvidam Brahma (Everything is, indeed, the Brahman)

Ekam Evadwitiyam (It is one, without a second)

Brahma Satyam, Jagan Mitya,
Jeevo Brahmaiva Naparah, says Adi Shankara. (Brahman alone is Truth, the world is unreal. The individual soul is the Brahman only and none other.)

Satyam Jnanam Anantam Brahmam (The Brahman is Truth, Knowledge and is Infinite & Eternal)

Aham Brahmasmi (I am the Brahman)

Tatvamasi [That (the Brahman) thou art]

Knowledge of the Jiva or the individual soul and the Brahman or the Supreme Soul cannot be reached purely through an intellectual exercise or study. The individual soul has to discard the three lower levels (the waking state, the dreaming state and the state of deep sleep) and reach the *turiya* or the superconscious state. This is reached only through spiritual enlightenment achieved by an all-pervading spiritual yearning which, after intense meditation, results in the realisation of the Jiva's oneness with the Brahman.

At this point, the Jnana Yogi becomes a Jivanmukta or liberated soul. Even though his soul is still in his body, it is now free and enjoys the eternal joy and bliss of the Brahman.

From Darkness towards Light

Hindus are the proud inheritors of timeless religious beliefs
leading to the traditions of the oldest religion in the world.
This faith has withstood the ravages of so many wars, when
the temples of the faith were destroyed and plundered, and
has survived widespread efforts to convert the members
of the faith to other religions.

Today it faces its greatest challenge as very few educated
Hindus of today know anything of their own religion. Because
of the lack of compulsion and the free thinking permitted in the
religion, which does not force a Hindu to visit a temple, attend
discourses on religion or even pray at home, this freedom
has resulted in license and, far worse, in ignorance which,
according to Hinduism, is the most undesirable of all vices
of Man.

The various incarnations of the Great God symbolically
fought the demon of ignorance and destroyed him. We may not
be able to persuade an incarnation of God to come down to the
earth to destroy this ignorance of ours, but we could be guided
by the practical dynamism of Lord Krishna, the philosophical
heights reached by Adi Shankara, and repeat
the song of the Upanishadic sages and pray with them, with
fearless hearts and an endless vision for all our
tomorrows . . . .

> From the unreal lead me to the Real,
> From darkness lead me to Light,
> From death lead me to Immortality.

OM SHANTIH SHANTIH SHANTIHI!
(OM PEACE, PEACE, PEACE!)

Glossary and Index of Pronunciations

All Indian words are spelt phonetically and their meanings are given in the text itself to avoid cross references to the glossary. However for the guidance of the visitor from abroad, a glossary of a few important words are given. The pronunciations are given, and where emphasis is to be placed, that part of the word is underlined. Wherever felt necessary, rhyming words are given (e.g. mun to rhyme with run) etc.

Local accents greatly influence pronunciations in different parts of India e.g. the Sanskrit Rama is pronounced Raam in the north and Raamaa in the south, the Sanskrit vishwa as bishwa in the east etc.

General guidelines for pronounciations are as follows:

a	should be pronounced as u in but
aa	as the extended a in the exclamation ah
ay	as a in day
o	as o in the exclamation oh
ow	as ow in cow
uh	as the second u in murmur
d	as th in there
th	as th in myth
i	as i in pit
u	as u in put

Word	Pronunciation	Meaning
Adharma	a-dhar-ma	That which is against the path of Righteousness
Advaita	ad-vy (to rhyme with my)-tha	A school of philosophy which says that God and Man are one, not two
Agama	aa-ga-ma	Doctrines and rituals of worship
Ahimsa	a-him-sa	Non-injury, non-violence
Apara bhakti	a-pa-raa bhuk (to rhyme with luck)-thi	Lower form of spiritual devotion
Ashram	aash-rum (to rhyme with sum)	Dwelling of a holy man
Ashrama	aash-ra-muh	One of the four stages in the life of a man
asura	a-su-ra	Demon personifying evil
Atma	aath-maa	The individual soul in each being
Atman	aath-mun (to rhyme with run)	The Great Soul. Another name for the Brahman, the Universal Spirit
Avatar	a-vuh-thaar	Incarnation of God on earth
Bhagavad Gita	Bha-ga-vad Gee-tha	The Song of the Lord, containing Lord Krishna's advice to Arjuna on the battlefield
Bhakta	bhuk (to rhyme with luck)-tha	A devotee
Bhakti	bhuk (to rhyme with luck)-thi	Spiritual devotion
Bhakti yoga	bhuk (to rhyme with luck)-thi yo-guh	The path to God through devotion
Brahma	brum (to rhyme with sum)-ha	The Creator in the Hindu Trinity
Brahmachari	brum (to rhyme with sum)-ha-chaa-ri	A student; also means a celibate
Brahman	brum (to rhyme with sum)-hun (to rhyme with sun)	The Great Soul, the Universal Spirit, the Absolute
Deva	day-vuh	A lesser god, a divine or celestial being
Dharma	dharr-ma	Law of Righteousness, one's righteous duty
Ganesha, Ganapati	ga-nay-shuh, ga-na-pa-thi	The son of Shiva and Parvati, the remover of obstacles
Gotra	go-thruh	Clan or family
Grihastha	gruh-hus (to rhyme with bus)-tha	A householder, a married man
Guru	gu-ru	Teacher, guide
Ishta Devata	ish-tuh day-vuh-tha	The deity chosen for personal worship by a devotee
Ishwara	eesh-wa-ra	The Great God
Itihasa	i-thi-haa-suh	The epics of Hinduism
Jiva	jee-va	The individual soul
Jivanmukta	jee-vun (to rhyme with run)-mook (to rhyme with book)-tha	One who attains God-head even while in this world, a liberated soul
Jnana yoga	gnyaa-nuh yo-guh	The path to God through spiritual knowledge
Kalpa	kull (to rhyme with hull)-puh	A day of Brahma equal to 4320 million earth years
Karma	karr-ma	One's actions, duty

82